Shaykhul Islā

Introduction to al-Fatwā al-Ḥamawiyyah

A Classical Work Clarifying the Orthodox Islāmic Belief Concerning Allāh's Names and Attributes and a Critique of those who Distort and Deny them and Revile the Understanding of the *Salaf*

Compiled and translated by Anwar Wright

First Edition: 1441H/November 2019CE

Cover: Usul Design

ISBN: 978-1-939833-09-9

Published by:
Sunnah Publishing
Grand Rapids MI, USA
Admin@SunnahPublishing.net

Visit us on the Web:
Http://www.SunnahPublishing.net
Http://www.MasjidSunnah.org
Http://www.SunnahAudio.com
Http://www.SalafiConference.com

Table of Contents

Transliteration Table

Consonants

ء	ʾ	د	**d**	ض	**ḍ**	ك	**k**
ب	**B**	ذ	**dh**	ط	**ṭ**	ل	**l**
ت	**T**	ر	**r**	ظ	**ẓ**	م	**m**
ث	**Th**	ز	**z**	ع	ʿ	ن	**n**
ج	**J**	س	**s**	غ	**gh**	ه	**h**
ح	**ḥ**	ش	**sh**	ف	**f**	و	**w**
خ	**Kh**	ص	**ṣ**	ق	**q**	ي	**y**

Vowels

Short	ـَ	**a**	ـِ	**i**	ـُ	**u**
Long	ـَا	**ā**	ـِي	**ī**	ـُو	**ū**

Diphthongs	ـَوْ	**aw**	ـَيْ	**ay**

عَزَّوَجَلَّ	The Mighty and Majestic.
سُبْحَانَهُۥوَتَعَالَىٰ	The Sublime and Exalted.
صَلَّىٱللَّهُعَلَيْهِوَسَلَّمَ	May Allāh make good mention of His Prophet in the highest company and grant him safety in this life and the next.
رَضِيَٱللَّهُعَنْهُ	May Allāh be pleased with him.
رَحِمَهُٱللَّهُ	May Allāh show mercy to him.
عَلَيْهِٱلسَّلَامُ	Peace be upon him.

بسم الله الرحمن الرحيم

Foreword

"...As to proceed; Indeed, Allāh (سُبْحَانَهُۥ وَتَعَالَىٰ) sent Muḥammad (صَلَّى ٱللَّٰهُ عَلَيْهِ وَسَلَّمَ) with guidance and the religion of truth as a mercy for all creation, as an example for those who perform righteous deeds, and as an authority over all of mankind. He carried out the task which he was entrusted with, conveyed the message, gave sincere advice to the *Ummah*, and thoroughly explained to the people everything that they are in need of, whether it be in the foundations or branches of the religion. There was no good except that he clarified and called to it, and no evil except that he warned the *Ummah* from it, up until he left them upon a clear white plain, its night is like its day. His Companions treaded upon it, [as it was] radiant and luminous, and the praiseworthy generations took it from them. [This matter remained as such] until times became overcast with the darkness of various innovations in which those who brought them used to plot against Islām and its people, to the extent individuals began to wander blindly [in those innovations] and built their belief system upon a flimsy premise.

However, Allāh (سُبْحَانَهُۥ وَتَعَالَىٰ) protects His religion by way of His close allies (*awliyā'*) upon whom He bestowed *īmān*, knowledge, and wisdom through which they are able to hinder these enemies and flip their plots back upon them. Therefore, no one has ever brought about an innovation except that Allāh decrees from among *Ahlus Sunnah* [one] who will demolish and refute that innovation, and to Him belongs all praise. At the forefront of those who repressed these innovators was Shaykh al-Islām Taqī al-Dīn Aḥmad Ibn 'Abd al-Ḥalīm Ibn 'Abd al-Salām Ibn Taymiyyah al-Ḥarrānī, al-Dimishqī, who was born in Ḥarrān on Monday, the 10th of *Rabī' al-Awwal*,

661H, and died in the year 728H in the month of *Dhū al-Qiʿdah*, while unjustly incarcerated in the Citadel of Damascus, may Allāh have mercy upon him.

He has numerous works in clarification of the *Sunnah* and cementing its foundations, and demolishing innovations.

From his works in this regard is the treatise "*al-Fatwā al-Ḥamawiyyah*" which he wrote in the year 698H in response to a question that was posed to him from Ḥamā, a town in Shām. In it he was asked about the statements of the jurists and Imāms of the religion concerning the verses and *aḥadīth* of [Allāh's] Attributes. He answered in a response of about eighty-three pages, and because of it he was put through trials and tribulations. May Allāh (سُبْحَانَهُ وَتَعَالَى) reward him on behalf of Islām and the Muslims with the best reward."[1]

Indeed, the treatise "*al-Fatwā al-Ḥamawiyyah*" is a tremendous gem for the person of *Sunnah* and *Salafī* creed, as it relates to the orthodox belief of the Muslims regarding the Names and Attributes of Allāh, just as it is a critique of those who went astray in this subject. This work is relevant and extremely important today, as we find the pupils and offshoots of the *Jahmiyyah*, such as the *Ashāʿirah* (i.e. *Ashʿaris*) and *Aḥbāsh*[2] (i.e. *Ḥabashis*) very active in the English speaking world, spreading their erroneous beliefs by denying and distorting the Attributes of Allāh, especially Allāh's Attribute of *al-ʿUluw* (His Highness above His creation), *al-Istiwā* (rising over His

---

[1] *Fatḥ Rabb al-Bariyyah bi Talkhīs al-Ḥamawiyyah* (p. 5-6) by Shaykh al-ʿUthaymīn (رَحِمَهُ ٱللَّهُ).

[2] **(TN):** Because of these circulating doubts, we previously translated the beneficial *Fatwā* from the Permanent Committee of Scholars in Saudi Arabia entitled: "The Misguidance of the Habashi Sect" and it is in print, and all praise is for Allāh.

throne), *al-Kalām* (His speech), and other Attributes. Rather, over the centuries, the two Attributes of Allāh, *al-'Uluw* and *al-Kalām*, have always been a matter of contention between the followers of the *Salaf*[1] and between the people of innovation. *Shaykh* Muḥammad Amān al-Jāmī (رَحِمَهُ ٱللَّهُ) stated in his explanation of *al-Fatwā al-Ḥamawiyyah*: "Why did Shaykh al-Islām begin with the Attribute of *al-'Uluw*? Because this Attribute, along with [Allāh's] Attribute of *Kalām*, has always been the subject of dispute between the *Khalaf*[2] and the followers of the *Salaf*. The majority of confusion and doubt of the *Khalaf* is concerning these two Attributes—*al-'Uluw* and *al-Kalām*—although their confusion and doubt concerning the Attribute of *al-'Uluw* is more. Perhaps they may even declare a disbeliever the one who affirms that Allāh is above. In some of the books of the *Ashā'irah*, it is asserted that whoever points [towards the sky] and believes that Allāh is above in His essence is a disbeliever, and whoever points [towards the sky] without holding that belief is a *fāsiq* (rebellious sinner)..."[3]

Hence, if Allāh wills this introduction will serve as a guide for the person of *Sunnah* and *Salafī* creed to understand the methodology of the *Salaf* in this subject, and refute and repel the doubts of the people of innovation and misguidance.

---

[1] **(TN):** The *Salaf* are the Companions [of the Prophet], the successors of the Companions (*Tābi'īn*), and those who follow them in goodness until the Day of Judgment from among those who the *Ummah* have agreed upon their integrity and righteousness, and have not been labelled with innovation that constitutes sin (*fisq*) or disbelief (*kufr*). See *al-Tuḥfah al-Siniyyah fī Bayān Maqāṣid al-Fatwā al-Ḥamawiyyah* (p. 113).

[2] **(TN):** The *Khalaf* are those who opposed the path of the Prophet (صَلَّى ٱللَّهُ عَلَيْهِ وَسَلَّمَ) and his Companions in matters of creed (*'aqīdah*), and everyone who came after the praiseworthy generations, treading the path of the innovators. See *al-Tuḥfah al-Siniyyah fī Bayān Maqāṣid al-Fatwā al-Ḥamawiyyah* (p. 158).

[3] (1/88-89).

As a prelude to this introduction we will mention what is meant by the *Tawḥīd* of Allāh's Names and Attributes, five ways a person deviates (*ilḥād*) concerning them, and also some beneficial questions and answers regarding the book *al-Fatwā al-Ḥamawiyyah* in order that the reader can become familiarized with it. Then we will mention the importance of this book and some of the most prevalent components that the text entails. This will be followed by the English text of the introduction of *Fatwā al-Ḥamawiyyah*, along with brief commentary from the explanations of two eminent scholars. The *'Allāmah*, Shaykh Ṣāliḥ al-Fawzān حفظه الله, from his book *al-Ta'līqāt al-Tawḍīḥiyyah 'alā al-Fatwā al-Ḥamawiyyah*—represented by the initials (SF)—and the explanation of the *'Allāmah*, Shaykh Muḥammad Amān al-Jamī (رَحِمَهُ اللَّهُ), represented by the initials (MA). Finally, we will conclude by mentioning its English text again without commentary followed by the Arabic text for those who wish to memorize it.

All footnotes labelled (TN) are from myself, the translator, and footnotes labelled (AI) are from our noble brother, *Ustādh* Abu Iyad Amjad Rafiq.

I ask Allāh, *al-'Alī al-'Aẓīm* (The Most High, The Most Great), *al-Samī', al-Mujīb* (The All-Hearer, The One who answers supplications), *al-Hādī*, (The One who Guides) to make this work a source of clarity and guidance for the Muslims and to keep us firm upon the *Qur'ān*, *Sunnah*, and the way of the *Salaf al-Ṣāliḥ* until we meet our Lord.

و صلى الله و سلم على نبينا محمد و على آله و صحبه و سلم

Written by Anwar Wright
8th night of *Dhū al-Ḥijjah*, 1440H, corresponding with August 8th 2019CE

Thanks and Gratitude

After thanking Allāh (سُبْحَانَهُ وَتَعَالَىٰ) for facilitating this translation and compilation, I then would like to thank the following people:

- Abu al-Hasan Mālik al-Akhdar who reviewed the translation of the text of *al-Fatwā al-Ḥamawiyyah* in its beginning stages and gave me priceless pointers and suggestions.

- Abu Iyad Amjad Rafiq who reviewed the entire book towards its end stages and offered many important suggestions, corrections, and brief footnotes.

- Abu Aasiyah Herrerah and his family for taking out of their busy schedules to edit the book.

- Maaz Qureshi who took from his valuable time to typeset the book, have a final review of the translation, and finally, print the book.

- My beloved wife and children who patiently endure my taking from their time in order to compile such works.

I ask Allāh to reward them all abundantly and to give them the good of this life and the Hereafter. *Āmīn.*

◈◈◈

Meaning of the Tawḥīd of Allāh's Names and Attributes (al-Asmā' wa al-Ṣifāt)[1]

It is to believe that Allāh is One with complete perfection from every aspect, [possessing] lofty, exalted, and beautiful Attributes. This [belief is actualized] by affirming the Names and Attributes He affirmed for Himself, or what His Messenger affirmed for Him, including their meanings and rulings that have been reported in the Book and *Sunnah*. Some examples are affirming that Allāh is All-Knowledgeable of all things (*al-'Alīm*), that He is All-Capable of doing all things (*al-Qadīr*), that He is the All Living, Self-Sustainer (*al-Ḥayy, al-Qayyūm*) who does not sleep nor slumber. Also, that He has a Will which will surely come to pass, [He has the] utmost divine Wisdom, He rose above His Throne (*Istawā*), and is with His servants wherever they are [through His Knowledge]. This [belief is held with the affirmation] that there is nothing similar to Him in His Essence, neither in His Attributes, nor in His Actions.

This type of *Tawḥīd* is the greatest thing one can have awareness of, as it entails having knowledge of Allāh through His Names and Attributes, and with this knowledge acts of worship are established. If the servant does not know his Lord, then how can he worship Him? How can one worship a Lord that they do not know? For this reason, the proofs and evidences that mention Him and laud Him [by way of His Names and Attributes] are plentiful, because the more important a matter is, the more one will find its clarification and explanation present.

---

[1] *Al-Tuḥfah al-Siniyyah fī Bayān Maqāṣid al-Fatwā al-Ḥamawiyyah* (p. 39) by Muḥammad Ibn 'Abd al-Raḥmān al-Khumayyis.

Matters that Violate Belief in Allāh's Names and Attributes[1]

Five things violate and desecrate this [category] of *Tawḥīd*, and all of them are types of *ilḥād* (deviation) regarding [Allāh's] Names; a matter which Allāh rebuked along with those who do it. He said (تَبَارَكَ وَتَعَالَى):

﴿وَلِلَّهِ ٱلْأَسْمَآءُ ٱلْحُسْنَىٰ فَٱدْعُوهُ بِهَا ۖ وَذَرُوا۟ ٱلَّذِينَ يُلْحِدُونَ فِىٓ أَسْمَـٰٓئِهِۦ ۚ سَيُجْزَوْنَ مَا كَانُوا۟ يَعْمَلُونَ ﴿١٨٠﴾﴾

"And all the Most Beautiful Names belong to Allāh, so call on Him by them, and leave the company of those who belie, or deny or utter impious speech against His Names. They will be requited for what they used to do."

[Sūrah al-Aʿrāf 7:180]

These things that violate [Allāh's Names and Attributes] are resembling Him [to His creation] (*Tashbīh*), denying them [*Taʿṭīl*), and naming and describing Him with that which does not befit Him. Ibn al-Qayyim said: *al-ilḥād* regarding the Names of Allāh is of different types:

One: Naming idols with [His] Names, such as those who named *al-Lāt* from *al-Ilāh* (The One True God), and *al-ʿUzzā* from *al-ʿAzīz* (the All-Mighty), and to call any idol *ilāh* (God).

---

[1] *Al-Tuḥfah al-Siniyyah fī Bayān Maqāṣid al-Fatwā al-Ḥamawiyyah* (p. 40), and the origin of this speech is summarized from Ibn al-Qayyim's speech in *Badāʾiʿ al-Fawāʾid*.

Two: Naming Him what does not befit His Majesty, such as how the Christians call Him Father, and how the Philosophers call Him: "The One whose essence makes the existence of the universe necessary (*Mūjib bi dhātihi*)" [1] and "the Efficient Cause (*'illatun fā'ilah*)."[2]

Three: Describing Him with deficiencies which He is high and far above, such as the statement of those evil ones among the Jews who said that He is poor, their statement that He rested after creating the creation, and that Allāh's Hand is tied up, etc.

Four: Stripping [His] Names of their [true] meanings and rejecting their realities, such as the statement of some of the *Jahmiyyah* and their followers that [His Names] are meaningless nouns which do not point to Attributes or [true] meanings.

Fifth: Resembling His Attributes to those of the creation. Glorified and Exalted is He above what the *Mushabbihūn* (i.e. Those who resemble Him to the creation) say.

◈◈◈

---

[1] (AI) This label is used by those such as Ibn Sīnā who claim the universe is eternal because its existence is necessitated by Allāh's existence.

[2] (AI) This refers to the being or the reason behind the existence of a thing.

Questions and Answers about the Book al-Fatwā al-Ḥamawiyyah[1]

[Q1]: Why has this treatise been named *al-Fatwā al-Ḥamawiyyah*?

[A1]: *al-Ḥamawiyyah* is an ascription to the town of the questioner which is Ḥamā, a city in Shām in the middle of Syria, north of Homs. It is known that the Shaykh did not initiate authoring this book, however it was an answer to a question that came to him from a student of knowledge who was confused about an issue regarding [Allāh's] Attributes, and in particular the Attributes which cannot be known except by way of the texts (i.e. *al-ṣifāt al-khabariyyah.*)[2] The

---

[1] *Al-Tuḥfah al-Siniyyah fī Bayān Maqāṣid al-Fatwā al-Ḥamawiyyah* (p. 91-95).

[2] **(TN):** "The Attributes which are not possible to affirm except by way of the texts [of *Qur'an* and *Sunnah*] are known as *al-ṣifāt al-khabariyyah,* and they are also known as "*al-khabariyyah al-maḥḍah*" (i.e. Attributes solely known by way of texts). As for the Attributes which can be affirmed by way of intellectual-proofs, along with affirming them by way of the texts, they sometimes may be called *al-ṣifāt al-ʿaqliyyah.* However, it is better that it be said of them: *ṣifāt khabariyyah ʿaqliyyah,* together. What is meant [by these Attributes] is that they are not solely known by way of texts. If [the word] *al-Khabariyyah* is used in an unrestricted sense, what is meant is those Attributes solely known by way of the texts, such as *al-Istiwā.* If no texts have been reported from Allāh or His Messenger (ﷺ) that Allāh rose (*Istawā*) above His throne, there would be no way for the intellect to know this Attribute. For this reason, they are known as *al-ṣifāt al-khabariyyah.* Likewise, *al-Majīʾ* - Allāh coming on the Day of Resurrection in order for the reckoning to begin, and *al-Nuzūl* -the Lord descending to the lowest heaven; all of these are known as *ṣifāt fiʿliyyah khabariyyah maḥḍah* (i.e. Attributes related to Allāh's actions which can only be known by way of the texts). There is also what is known as *ṣifāt khabariyyah dhātiyyah* (i.e. Attributes related to Allāh's Essence which only can be known by way of texts), such as affirming the attribute of *al-Wajh* (Allāh's Face), *al-Yadayn* (Allāh's two Hands), *al-Qadam* (Allāh's Foot), and *Aṣābiʿ* (Allāh's Fingers). These are known as *khabariyyah dhātiyyah.* Therefore, the *ṣifāt al-*

questioner was from the city of Ḥamā, thus the book took on this name, being attributed to the city of the questioner.

[Q2]: When did Shaykh al-Islām author *al-Fatwā al-Ḥamawiyyah*?

[A2]: Shaykh al-Islām authored this treatise when he was less than forty years of age, in the beginning of the month of *Rabī' al-Awwal* in the year 698H, between the *Dhuhr* and *'Asr* prayers.

---

khabariyyah are of two categories: *khabariyyah fi'liyyah* (i.e. Attributes only known by way of the texts that relate to Allāh's actions), such as *al-Istiwā*, *al-Nuzūl*, *al-Majī'*, and [the second is] *khabariyyah dhātiyyah* (i.e. Attributes only known by way of the texts that relate to Allāh's Essence), such as *al-Wajh*, *al-Yadain*, *al-Qadam*, *al-Aṣābi'*, *al-'Ayn*, and *al-Nafs*. These are some of the Attributes which are *khabariyyah dhātiyyah* and can only be known by way of the texts. As for affirming, for example, the Attributes of *al-Sam'* (Hearing), and *al-Baṣr* (Seeing), *Ahl al-Kalām* who affirm these Attributes, meaning the *Ashā'irah* [in particular] call [these Attributes] *al-ṣifāt al-'aqliyyah* (i.e. Attributes which can be known by way of intellect), and they are the *al-ṣifāt al-Ma'ānī* which are well known among them. However, we [*Ahlus Sunnah*] call them conjointly: *al-ṣifāt al-khabariyyah al-'aqliyyah*. Meaning, if no texts have been reported that Allah is *al-Qadīr* (the All Capable), and that He is *al-Murīd* (He has a Will and Want), and that He is All Hearing, and All Seeing, and the He is All Knowing, and All Wise, the intellect would still point to them by using the universal-signs [of Allah] as evidence, and likewise [what we witness from] this extraordinary precision [in the universe]. The fact that things come into existence and are removed from existence shows the Attribute of *al-Qudrah* (Allah's ability), as well as the Attribute of *'ilm* (His knowledge), and *al-Ḥayāt* (His Perfect life). And the fact that certain things are specified [in particular ways], this shows both the Attributes of *'ilm* (Allāh's Knowledge) and *Irādah* (Allāh's Will and Want). Further, this marvelous origination of creation [we see] not being preceded by anything similar - because Allah is the Originator of the Heavens and Earth- shows that [He has] the utmost divine Wisdom (*al-Ḥikmah*), and remarkable capability (*al-Qudrah*). Therefore, these are called conjointly: *al-ṣifāt al-khabariyyah al-'aqliyyah...*" Refer to *Sharḥ al-Fatwā al-Ḥamawiyyah* (1/305-306) by Shaykh Muḥammad Amān al-Jāmī.

[Q3]: What is the subject of the book?

[A3]: The subject of the book is:

1- To affirm the Attributes [of Allāh] that were reported in the Book and the *Sunnah*, and in particular the *ṣifāt al-khabariyyah*.

2- To establish what the methodology of the *Salaf* is regarding [Allāh's] Attributes and mentioning their speech [regarding that]. Shaykh al-Islām stated, "The purpose behind this answer is to mention the sayings of some of the Imāms [of the religion] who have conveyed the methodology of the *Salaf* in this subject."

3- To refute the methodology of the opposers from among those who ascribe to the *Sunnah*, but at the same time they deny the *ṣifāt al-khabariyyah*, such as the *Ashā'irah*, the *Māturīdiyyah*,[1] and others who claim that the way of the *Salaf* is safer while the way of the *Khalaf* is more knowledgeable and more precise.

[Q4]: Speak about the importance of the treatise "*al-Ḥamawiyyah*."

[A4]: The importance of *al-Fatwā al-Ḥamawiyyah* goes back to the following matters:

1- [It shows] the importance of the issue that has been inquired about, which is the Attributes [of Allāh], and in particular the *ṣifāt al-khabariyyah*.

---

[1] **(TN):** A sect of *Ahl al-Kalām* and is an ascription to Abū Manṣūr al-Māturīdī (d.333H)

2- [It clarifies] the great number of people who have become immersed in this issue with false speech from among *Ahl al-Kalām*[1] and others.

3- [It brings to light] the great number of doubts which the opposition raised in this subject, which resulted in them falling into various types of misguidance.

4- It is a refutation against *Ahl al-Kalām* and the deviant sects [who have strayed] in this subject from the people who ascribe ignorance to the *Salaf* (*Ahl al-Tajhīl*), and the people who reinterpret the Attributes of Allāh with false interpretations (*Ahl al-Taʿwīl*).

5- It refutes the claim of the *Ashāʿirah* and *Ahl al-Kalām* that the way of the *Khalaf* is more knowledgeable and more precise than the way of the *Salaf*.

[Q5]: What is the objective of the treatise "*al-Ḥamawiyyah*" and what are the benefits obtained [from studying it]?

[A5]: The objective and benefits obtained from *al-Ḥamawiyyah* are the following:

---

[1] **(TN):** They are those who relied upon speculative theology (*ʿilm al-kalām*) and claimed that the evidences for belief in Allāh and affirmation or negation of His Names and Attributes return to the intellect and principles of logic. They hold these "evidences" and principles to be certainties, while they hold knowledge of the Book and the *Sunnah* to be based upon speculative evidences. Due to this, they give precedence to their intellects over the texts of the Book and *Sunnah*. Their statements began to appear during the end of the era of the *Tābiʿīn*, and then became widespread after the three [praiseworthy] generations. After the books of the Romans and Greeks were translated into the Arabic language, the tribulations that occurred because of *ʿilm al-kalām* became even worse. See *Sharḥ Fatḥ Rabb al-Bariyyah bi Talkhīṣ al-Ḥamawiyyah* (p. 533-534) by Shaykh al-ʿUthaymīn (رَحِمَهُ ٱللَّهُ).

1- It destroys the methodology of the *Khalaf* and clarifies its falsehood; this is because they treaded two paths:

a- The path of *Tafwīḍ* [treaded by] *Ahl al-Tajhīl*,[1] and this occurred by them ascribing ignorance to the Companions and the *Salaf*.

b- The path of reinterpreting [Allāh's Attributes] (*Ta'wīl*) and this is by distorting them [from their true meanings]. Due to this they have stated: "The way of the *Salaf* is safer, while the way of the *Khalaf* is more knowledgeable and more precise." The author has refuted this false claim at length.

2- It shows the correctness of the way of the *Salaf*, that it is safer, more knowledgeable, and more precise.

[Q6]: Mention some of the explanations of *al-Fatwā al-Ḥamawiyyah.*

[A6]: *al-Fatwā al-Ḥamawiyyah* has a few concise explanations which are:

1- *al-Kawākib al-Durriyyah*, which is the commentary of *al-'Allāmah* 'Abd al-'Azīz Ibn Bāz (رَحِمَهُ ٱللَّهُ) on *al-Ḥamawiyyah.*
2- *al-Ta'līqāt al-Tawḍīḥiyyah 'alā al-Fatwā al-Ḥamawiyyah* by *al-'Allāmah* Ṣāliḥ al-Fawzān حفظه الله.

[1] See previous question.

3- *Fatḥ Rabb al-Bariyyah bi Talkhīs al-Ḥamawiyyah*, by al-ʿAllamah Muḥammad Ibn Ṣāliḥ al-ʿUthaymīn (رَحِمَهُ ٱللَّهُ). In this book the Shaykh summarized *al-Ḥamawiyyah.*[1]

[Q7]: Is the treatise "*al-Ḥamawiyyah*" a book written to explain the matters of *ʿAqīdah* or is it a book which entails a refutation upon the way of the people of opposition?

[A7]: 1- It is a book written to explain the *ʿAqīdah* of the *Salaf* in the subject of [Allāh's] Attributes and in particular the *ṣifāt al-khabariyyah.* [Shaykh al-Islām] presented that by mentioning evidences from the Book and *Sunnah*, as well as by presenting the statements of some of the Imāms [of the religion] who conveyed the methodology of the *Salaf* and their unanimous agreement [in this subject].

2- It is also a book that entails a refutation upon the way of the opposers, such as the *Ashāʿirah* and others. For this reason, he refuted them by mentioning the statements of *Ahl al-Kalām* themselves from among the *Ashāʿirah* who affirm [Allāh's] Attributes, like Abū al-Ḥasan al-Ashʿarī, Abū Māʿalī al-Juwaynī, or those who were affected by them such as al-Bayhaqī and Abū Yaʿlā. He also mentioned those who ascribe to the *Ṣufi* path [who affirm these Attributes], such as ʿUmar Ibn Aḥmad al-Asbāhānī, ʿAmr Ibn ʿUthmān al-Makkī, al-Ḥārith al-Muḥāsibī, Muḥammad Ibn Khafīf, Muḥammad Ibn ʿAbd al-Qādir al-Jīlānī, and others.

[Q8]: What is the difference between *al-Fatwā al-Ḥamawiyyah* and *al-Wāsiṭiyyah*?

---

[1] **(TN):** There is another explanation of *al-Fatwā al-Ḥamawiyyah* recently printed from the lessons of *al-ʿAllāmah* Muḥammad Amān al-Jāmī (رَحِمَهُ ٱللَّهُ), and we have included some of its commentary.

[A8]: There is a great difference between *al-Ḥamawiyyah* and *al-Wāsiṭiyyah* as it relates to the names and the subject matter. The clarification is as follows:

1- As for the title, *al-Wāsiṭiyyah* is an ascription to the town of the questioner which is Wāsiṭ, in Irāq. *al-Ḥamawiyyah* is an ascription to the town of the questioner, Ḥamā in Shām (Syria).

2- As far as it relates to the subject matter, then *al-Wāsiṭiyyah* is a book that explains the *'Aqīdah* of the saved, victorious sect up until the hour is established, *Ahl al-Sunnah wa al-Jamā'ah*, in matters of belief such as *īmān*, resurrection (*ba'th*), divine decree (*al-Qadar*), Attributes (*al-Ṣifāt*), miracles of the *awliyā* (*al-Karāmāt*), [the correct belief] regarding the Companions, and other matters.

As for the subject of *al-Ḥamawiyyah*, it is regarding [Allāh's] attributes [only], especially the *ṣifāt al-khabariyyah*, and it refutes the way of the opposers [in this matter].

3- As for the manner in which the author explained [these books] and the methodology that he traversed upon, then *al-Ḥamawiyyah* is distinguished by mentioning evidences from the Book and the *Sunnah* while mentioning a myriad of quotes from the scholars of the *Salaf*, *Ahl al-Kalām* from among the *Ashā'irah*, as well as the people of *Taṣawwuf* (i.e. *Ṣufis)*. [The author did this] in order to compel the opposition to accept the truth (i.e. as even some from those groups affirmed the Attributes of Allāh in a manner befitting His Majesty).
As for *al-Wāsiṭiyyah*, the author sufficed with presenting the foundations of *Ahl al-Sunnah* along with mentioning the evidences from the Book and *Sunnah*.

[Q9]: What was the stance of the opposition towards *al-Fatwā al-Ḥamawiyyah*?

[A9]: This *Fatwā* resulted in many rebuttals, and Shaykh al-Islām was put through great tribulations as a result of it. The stances of the opposition manifested in the following:

1- Defaming the Shaykh, degrading him, tarnishing his reputation, and accusing him of matters he was innocent of, which is the norm of the people of innovation in every time.

2- Going to the judges and governors so they can prevent the Shaykh [from speaking], and so they may rule that his *ʿAqīdah* is false. He was summoned to the courts; however, Allāh kept him firm and aided him over his enemies.

3- Some books and treatises were authored in response to this *Fatwā* in order to refute what was mentioned in it, to cast doubts surrounding it, and to cast doubts within the people concerning it.

[Q11]: Mention some books that give importance to transmitting the methodology of the *Salaf*?[1]

[A11]: The books that give importance to transmitting the methodology of the *Salaf* are many and various, the most important being:

1- *Sharḥ Uṣūl al-Iʿtiqād Ahl al-Sunnah wa al-Jamāʿah* by Imām al-Lālikaʾī (d.418H)
2- *al-Ibānah* by Ibn al-Baṭṭah (d.378H)
3- *al-Sunnah* by al-Khallāl (d.311H)

[1] *Al-Tuḥfah al-Siniyyah fī Bayān Maqāṣid al-Fatwā al-Ḥamawiyyah* (p. 121).

4- *al-Tawḥīd* by Ibn Khuzaymah (d.311H)
5- *al-Raddu ʿalā al-Jahmiyyah* by al-Dārimī (d.280H)
6- *al-Sunnah* by ʿAbdullāh Ibn al-Imām Aḥmad (d.290H)
7- *al-Sunnah* by Abū Bakr Ibn Abū ʿĀṣim (d.287H)
8- *Khalq Afʿāl al-ʿIbād* by Abū ʿAbdullāh al-Bukhārī (d.256H)
9- *al-Radd ʿalā al-Jahmiyyah* by Imām Aḥmad (d.241H)
10- *al-Sharīʿah* by al-Ājurrī (d.360H)

◈◈◈

The Importance of this Introduction

Shaykh Muḥammad Amān al-Jāmī (رَحِمَهُ ٱللَّهُ) said regarding this introduction: "It is flames of fire against the *Mu'aṭṭilah*[1]..."

Shaykh Ṣāliḥ al-Fawzān says: "I chose to suffice with spreading the introduction because of the tremendous principles it entails, and because of [Ibn Taymiyyah's] statement: 'I only began with this introduction because the one who firmly understands it will know where the path of guidance lies in this subject, and other than it...[2]'"

"He began with this introduction which is called *Muqaddimah al-Ḥamawiyyah*. It is a tremendous introduction which the students of knowledge would memorize and give importance to due to it entailing clear principles by which the student of knowledge benefits from. Likewise, it clearly distinguishes between the knowledge of the *Salaf* and the knowledge of the *Khalaf*. Verily, the path of guidance is what the *Salaf* of this *ummah* were upon, and the path of misguidance is what the majority of the *Khalaf* were upon."[3]

"And this introduction entails many important matters, the most notable are the following:

One: What is obligatory towards [Allāh's] Names and Attributes is to tread upon the way of the *Salaf* from the Companions, the *Tābi'īn*

---

[1] *Sharḥ al-Fatwā al-Ḥamawiyyah al Kubrā* (1/84).

(TN): Shaykh al-'Uthaymīn stated, "The *Mu'aṭṭil* (i.e. singular form of *Mu'aṭṭilah*) is one who denies anything from Allāh's Names and Attributes, such as the *Jahmiyyah, Mu'tazilah, Ashā'irah*, et. al." *Fatḥ Rabb al-Bariyyah bi Talkhīs al-Ḥamawiyyah* (p. 81).

[2] *al-Ta'līqāt al-Tawḍīḥiyyah 'alā al-Fatwā al-Ḥamawiyyah* (p. 18).

[3] *al-Ta'līqāt al-Tawḍīḥiyyah 'alā al-Fatwā al-Ḥamawiyyah* (p. 78).

and the Imāms [of guidance] who came after them, and this is by affirming them just as they have been reported [to us] without distorting them (*taḥrīf*), negating them (*taʿṭīl*), asking how they occur (*takyīf*), and without resembling them [to the creation] (*tamthīl*).

Two: The *way* of the *Salaf* is safer, more knowledgeable, and more precise than the way of the *Khalaf*.

Three: The *Salaf* [themselves] are more knowledgeable than the *Khalaf*.

Four: There are some from among the *Khalaf* who recanted and retracted, then adhered to the way of the *Salaf* once the falsehood that they were upon became apparent to them, while others from them remained in their state of confusion.

Fifth: The way of the *Khalaf* entails ascribing ignorance to the *Salaf*, or deeming them as misguided, [just as it entails] explaining the texts away from their proper meaning (*ta'wīl*).

Sixth: The way of the *Salaf* is taken from the Messenger of Allāh, while the way of the *Khalaf* is taken from the *Jahmiyyah*, and the *Jahmiyyah* took [their way] from the Jews.

Seventh: The *Salaf* use the Book and *Sunnah* as evidence and they give precedence to the text over the intellect, while the *Khalaf* use principles of philosophical-logic and speculative theology as evidence, and they give precedence to the intellect over the text.

Eighth: The sound unpolluted intellect does not contradict sound authentic text.

Ninth: The *Bāṭinī*[1] heretics have argued [in refutation] against those who explain the Attributes [of Allāh] away from their apparent meanings, that [their metaphorical-interpretation of] the prayer, *zakāt*, and the affairs of the Hereafter [away from their apparent meanings] is similar to how the *Mu'aṭṭilah* reinterpret the Attributes [of Allāh], or even less severe. So why do [the *Mu'aṭṭilah*] reject the interpretation of the *Bāṭinīs*, when they are worse than them [in regards to their false interpretation]?

Tenth: The followers of the *Salafī* methodology are in agreement as it relates to the Names and Attributes because they followed the Book and *Sunnah*. As for the followers of the *Khalaf*, they are disunited among themselves because they follow speculative theology and principles of philosophical-logic.

Eleventh: The calamity that occurred [in the *Ummah*] as it relates to the *'aqīdah* stemmed from the translation of the books of the Romans into Arabic during the era of al-Ma'mūn al-'Abbāsī. At the same time, he was affected by evil advisors in his circle such as Bishr Ibn Ghiyāth al-Mirrīsī and Ibn Abī Du'ād."[2]

◈◈◈

---

[1] **(TN):** They were called *Bāṭinīyyah* (i.e. *Bāṭinīs*) because they claim that the Islāmic text (i.e. *Qur'ān* and *Sunnah*) has an outward apparent meaning (*Dhāhir*), as well as an inner hidden meaning (*Bāṭin*). They claim that the outward meaning of the text is intended for the layman, but as for those who attain the level of having knowledge of the "hidden meanings" [of the text], they are then absolved from performing all obligations... See footnote of *al-Fatwā al-Ḥamawiyyah* (p. 273), checking of Ḥamad al-Tuwajirī.

[2] *al-Ta'līqāt al-Tawḍīḥiyyah 'alā al-Fatwā al-Ḥamawiyyah* (p. 18-19).

The English Text of the Introduction to al-Fatwā al-Ḥamawiyyah With Commentary

In the year 698H, the great scholar Shaykh al-Islām Taqī al-Dīn Abū al-ʿAbbās Aḥmad Ibn ʿAbd al-Ḥalīm Ibn ʿAbd al-Salām Ibn Taymiyyah was asked [this question][1], and because of [his] answer,

---

[1] **(SF):** "The [questioner] asked him about the verses and *aḥādīth* reported concerning [Allāh's] Names and Attributes, as people began to talk, dispute and have doubt regarding them. From them were those who negated all [of Allāh's] Names and Attributes, such as the *Jahmiyyah*, and others negated [only] the Attributes, such as the *Muʿtazilah*. There were also those who negated most of the Attributes, and others distorted their meanings by explaining them away from their true meanings. This is because when they saw that they were unable to outright deny the texts, they resorted to negating their meanings and then added to them false interpretations. Others have stated that [His Attributes] are from the unclear texts (*Mutashābih*) and only Allāh knows their meanings. [They said] we read the words, but we do not explain them, rather we consider them to be from the unclear verses. These people are known as the *Mufawwiḍah*, and those [mentioned] before them are known as the *Muʿawwillah* (i.e. those who distort the Names and Attributes), and the *Muʿaṭṭilah* (i.e. those who deny the Names and Attributes). There is another group who exaggerated in affirming the [Attributes] to the extent that they resembled them to the Attributes of the creation, and they are known as the *Mumaththilah* and the *Mushabbihah*. As for *Ahl al-Sunnah wa al-Jamāʿah*, they affirmed them [the Names and Attributes] as well as their meanings in their correct context. They did not distort them nor explain them away [from their proper meanings], neither did they say that they are from the unclear text. They say that they are from the unambiguous, clear texts which meanings are known; however, the exact nature of how they occur (*al-kayfiyyah*) is unknown…Further, they did not say that they resemble the Attributes of the creation, but rather they said they are [Attributes] befitting Allāh. This is what the Companions, the *Tābiʿīn*, and those who followed them in goodness were upon. This was also the methodology of the leading [scholars] who came after them…" (p. 20-21)

matters [of hearings, judgments] and tribulations transpired.[1] It is an answer containing tremendous benefit.

The questioner asked:

What is the statement of the pre-eminent Scholars, the Imams of the Religion, regarding the verses containing the Attributes (*ṣifāt*) [of Allāh], such as His statement (عَزَّوَجَلَّ),

﴿ ٱلرَّحْمَٰنُ عَلَى ٱلْعَرْشِ ٱسْتَوَىٰ ۝٥ ﴾

> **"The Most Beneficent** (Allāh) **rose over** (*Istawā*) **the throne,"** [Sūrah Tā Hā 20:5]

And His statement (عَزَّوَجَلَّ),

﴿ ثُمَّ ٱسْتَوَىٰٓ إِلَى ٱلسَّمَآءِ وَهِىَ دُخَانٌ ﴾

> **"Then He rose over** (*Istawā*) **towards the heavens when it was smoke,"**
>
> [Sūrah al-Fuṣṣilat 41:11][2]

---

[1] **(SF):** "After this answer appeared, tribulations took place and the Shaykh was tried because of it and was summoned to court. When they could not overcome him by way of knowledge, they resorted to imprisoning him… However, all praise is for Allāh, they did not achieve what they wanted. They only gained humiliation and lowliness and the truth prevailed, though they hated it..." (p. 21)

[2] **(SF):** "Among the verses containing [Allāh's] Attributes which were misunderstood [by some] is the issue of [Allāh's] *Istiwā* over His throne. Allāh informed of Himself that He *Istawā* (rose) over the throne in seven places in His Book, all of them saying, "He rose over (*Istawā*) the throne." This proves that this *Istiwā* is real. It does not mean *Istīlā* (i.e conquered) as was stated by

And other verses and *aḥādīth* containing [His] Attributes, such as his saying (ﷺ), "Verily the hearts of the children of Ādam are between two Fingers from the Fingers of the Most Merciful," and his saying, "*Al-Jabbār*[1] [i.e. Allāh] will place His Foot in the Hell-Fire...,"[2] and similar *aḥādīth* [of this sort], and what do the scholars say [regarding them]? [Please] give a detailed answer regarding that, and may you be rewarded, if Allāh wills.[3]

[*Shaykh al-Islām*] answered:

---

the people of innovation. They say that "He rose (*Istawā*) over the throne" means that He conquered (*Istawlā*) the throne. They added the letter "*Lām*" in the Book of Allāh from their own selves, just as the Jews added a *Nūn* in the Torah. When it was said to [the Jews],

﴿وَقُولُوا حِطَّةٌ﴾

"Say ḥiṭṭah..." [Sūrah *al-Baqarah* 2:58]

Meaning, remove from us our sins, instead they said *ḥinṭa*, adding the letter *Nūn*. Their intent was food (i.e. as *ḥinṭa* is a type of wheat) and not to seek forgiveness. So the Jews added the letter *Nūn* in the Book of Allāh, and these [*Mu'awwilah*] added a *Lām* in the Book of Allāh. They said *Istawā* means *Istawlā*, [however] there has not been reported in the *Qur'ān* even one verse with the word *Istawlā*. This proves that this interpretation is false and rejected." (p. 22-23)

[1] **(TN):** The Compeller

[2] **(SF):** "This affirms a Foot for Allāh, according to what befits His majesty...We affirm this *ḥadīth* just as it has come to us and we do not try to involve our limited comprehension and intellects, thus we negate for Allāh what He has affirmed for Himself." (p. 24)

[3] **(MA):** "The word *In Shā' Allāh* (if Allāh wills) is not used when supplicating except if a person desires emphasis. The origin is that *In Shā' Allāh* is used [to show that a matter] is contingent [upon the will of Allāh]. It also can be used for emphasis, and this is what is intended here." (1/29)

All praise is due to Allāh, Lord of all creation. Our statement regarding [those texts containing Allāh's Attributes] is what Allāh and His Messenger have stated, as well as what was stated by the early Muslims who embraced Islām from the *Muhājirūn*, the *Anṣār*, and those who followed them in goodness, and the rightly guided Imāms after them; those whom the Muslims agree were rightly guided and possessed correct understanding. This is what is incumbent upon all people as it relates to this subject and other than it.[1]

Indeed, Allāh sent Muḥammad (ﷺ) with guidance and the true Religion, in order to remove mankind from [layers of] darkness into light, by the permission of their Lord, to the path of the All-Mighty, One Full of Praise. [Allāh] testified that He sent him as a

---

[1] **(SF):** "This is what is obligatory upon you as it relates to all affairs of the religion, and especially pertaining to the verses and *aḥādīth* of [Allāh's] Attributes. You say what Allāh said, what His Messenger said, and what was said by the *Muhājirūn*, the *Anṣār*, and those who followed them in exactness. Whoever opposes this is from the people of misguidance, deviation and they are astray. Therefore, it is incumbent upon you in the subject of [Allāh's] Names and Attributes, in the subject of *Tawḥīd* and *ʿaqīdah*, and in the religion in general that you follow this foundation, which is the methodology of the pious predecessors from among the *ṣaḥābah*, the *Tābiʿīn*, and the rightly guided Imāms. Do not stray from this [path] or claim that you have been given something which they have not attained, or that your understanding is better than theirs. Some people come with things from their own selves which the *Salaf* never said, nor the people of knowledge. They come with explanations and independent deductions (*ijtihādāt*) from their own selves regarding the foundation of *Tawḥīd*, which does not allow independent deductions. You have only been ordered with following (*al-ittibāʿ*). You say what the *Salaf* said and you refrain from what they refrained from, because they were more knowledgeable than you, and more grounded than you. Therefore, it suffices that you be one who follows them…" (p. 29)

caller to [his Lord] by His permission, and [sent him] as an illuminating lamp. He commanded him to say,

﴿ قُلْ هَٰذِهِۦ سَبِيلِىٓ أَدْعُوٓا۟ إِلَى ٱللَّهِ ۚ عَلَىٰ بَصِيرَةٍ أَنَا۠ وَمَنِ ٱتَّبَعَنِى ﴾

"This is my path. I call to Allāh upon certain knowledge, I and whosoever follows me."
[Sūrah Yūsuf 12:108]

Therefore, it is impossible intellectually and religiously that this illuminating lamp (i.e. Muḥammad) whom Allāh sent in order to remove the people from [layers of] darkness into light, and revealed to him the Book (i.e. *Qur'ān*) in order to judge between the people in which they differ, just as He commanded the people to return disputes in their religion back to the Book and Wisdom (*ḥikmah*) which he was sent with, along with [the Prophet] calling to Allāh and to His path upon certain knowledge, by [Allāh's] permission, and He informed that He completed for him and his *Ummah* their religion, and perfected His favor upon them; it is impossible alongside this and other [considerations] that [the Prophet(ﷺ)] left the subject of belief in Allāh and of knowledge regarding Him confusing and ambiguous,[1] not having distinguished between what is incumbent for Allāh of beautiful Names and lofty Attributes, what is permitted for Him [of actions], and what is impossible for Him[2].

---

[1] **(MA):** "This is logically impossible, and Islāmically impermissible. Had this been the case, he could not be [described] as one who had completely conveyed [the message]." (1/41)

[2] **(MA):** "We must understand these three headings; [**What is incumbent for Allah]:** That Allāh possesses complete perfection as it relates to [His] Names and Attributes. [**What is impossible for Him]**: [Meaning], those things which are impossible for him, [which are] the opposites of these Attributes [of

perfection]; Attributes opposite to knowledge, or hearing, or seeing, or Highness. These matters are impossible [for Allāh]. Also, such as [Him having] a partner, a wife, one who He is affectionately adores, or a helper; these matters are impossible for Allāh. **[And what is permitted for Him (of actions)]**: Meaning, what is permissible concerning Allāh, such as bringing matters into and out of existence, and giving and withholding. There is nothing obligatory upon Allāh. Allāh gives out of His benevolence and withholds out of [His] Justice, bestows guidance out of His grace and misguides due to [His justice]. He withholds, gives, raises [some] and lowers [others]; [He does] all of that. The servants constantly revolve between Allāh's grace and His justice. Therefore, there is nothing obligatory upon Allāh, and it cannot be imagined regarding Allāh that He is oppressive, ever. However, [matters] always revolve between [His] justice and [His] benevolence." (1/37-38).

(AI): In explanation of what is "*wājib*" (incumbent) for Allāh, Shaykh Muḥammad Amān clarified that with respect to His essence, Names and Attributes, perfections are incumbent for Him. Thus, knowledge, power, hearing, seeing and all other Attributes of perfection are incumbent for Allāh, and their opposites (ignorance, incapacity etc.), as well as deficiencies are impossible for Him. However, with respect to Allāh's actions, we cannot say anything is incumbent upon Him except what He made incumbent upon Himself, such as mercy, or made unlawful upon Himself such as oppression. This opposes the claim of the *Mu'tazilah* who say that it is incumbent upon Allāh to do whatever is in the best interests of the servants, a doctrine known as "*as-ṣāliḥ wa al-aṣlāh*." This is not true because Allāh misguides people and also punishes people, and neither of these are in their best interests. Rather, Allāh acts out of His justice (*'adl*) or His bounty (*faḍl*), and nothing is obligatory upon Him except what He makes obligatory upon Himself. Shaykh Muḥammad Amān alluded to this by saying that no one can make anything obligatory upon Allāh with respect to His actions. Shaykh al-Islām Ibn Taymiyyah said: "As for making something incumbent upon Him, the Sublime and Exalted, and making something unlawful for Him, by analogizing [for Him] with His creation, then this is the saying of the *Qadariyyah* and it is an innovated statement which opposes authentic reports and sound reason. *Ahl al-Sunnah* are agreed that He, the Sublime, is the Creator, Lord and Master of everything and that whatever He wills occurs and whatever He does not will does not occur. And that the servants cannot obligate anything upon Him. And as for those from *Ahl al-Sunnah* who did speak of (things being) obligatory

Surely, knowledge of [these matters] is the foundation of the religion and the basis of guidance.[1] It is also the best thing the hearts can acquire, what the souls can achieve, and what the intellects can comprehend. Therefore, how can that Book (i.e. *Qur'ān*), that Messenger (i.e. Muḥammad), and the best of mankind after the Prophets (i.e. the Companions) not completely master this subject in respect to belief and statement?[2] It is also impossible that the Prophet (ﷺ) taught his *Ummah* everything, even the

---

upon Him, they said: 'He prescribed mercy upon Himself and made oppression unlawful upon Himself' [on the basis of texts], and not [from the angle] that the servant deserves anything from Allāh [as if He is obligated to do something for His servants], similar to when one from the creation has a right over another." *Iqtiḍā' Ṣirāt al-Mustaqīm* (2/310). Thus, we can speak of perfections being incumbent (*wājib*) for Allāh in His Names and Attributes but we cannot speak of actions being incumbent upon Allāh, except what He made incumbent upon Himself. Allāh is not obligated with anything, and all of His actions are either from His justice or His benevolence. Through this, the two senses in which the word "*wājib*" has been used should be clear.

[1] **(SF):** "Knowledge of the *'aqīdah* is the foundation of the religion, so whoever is deficient in it is deficient in the religion itself. This is because if the foundation of a matter is weak, what is built upon it will not be stable. For example, if the foundation of a building becomes weak it will collapse, but if it is strong the building will stand upright...Therefore, how could the Messenger not give importance to the *'aqīdah* which is the foundation of the religion, and [not] explain and clarify it to the people?" (p. 41)

[2] **(SF):** "What preceded was a prelude and this is the result of the Shaykh's speech...how could the Book and *Sunnah* not clarify the correct *'aqīdah*? And how could [the Companions] not know the subject of [Allāh's] Names and Attributes by way of belief, statement, and action? This is a refutation against those who accuse the Companions of not knowing the meanings of these Names and Attributes, while Jahm Ibn Ṣafwān and those like him were the only ones who knew their meanings and clarified them. Before they were ambiguous [as they claim], and not known by the people, and those who came [before] only uttered words that they did not understand. Free is Allāh from all imperfections." (p. 44-45)

etiquettes of cleaning themselves [after using the bathroom[1]]—and said: "I have left you upon a clear white plain, its night is like its day, no one strays from it except that he is destroyed." There occurs in another authentic report, "Allāh never sent a Messenger except it was a duty upon him to point his *Ummah* to every good that he knew for them, and to warn them from every evil that he knew would harm them."[2] And Abū Dharr (رَضِيَ اللَّهُ عَنْهُ) said, "The Messenger of Allāh (صَلَّى اللَّهُ عَلَيْهِ وَسَلَّمَ) passed away, and there was not even a bird who flaps its wings in the sky except that he mentioned to us some knowledge concerning it," and ʿUmar Ibn Khaṭṭāb (رَضِيَ اللَّهُ عَنْهُ) said: "The Messenger of Allāh (صَلَّى اللَّهُ عَلَيْهِ وَسَلَّمَ) stood among us [one day] and mentioned the matters of the very beginning of creation all the way until the people of Paradise enter their dwellings, and the people of the Hell-Fire enter their dwellings. Those who memorized it did so,

---

[1] **(SF):** "How could he (صَلَّى اللَّهُ عَلَيْهِ وَسَلَّمَ) leave the subject of ʿ*aqīdah* not clarified to the people while it is the most important thing? The Messenger did not leave anything that was a benefit for the people in their religion except that he clarified it. Those who knew it did, and those who did not know it, simply did not. The Messenger (صَلَّى اللَّهُ عَلَيْهِ وَسَلَّمَ) did not pass away until the religion and the clarification were complete. The perfected legislation came from Allāh and the complete clarification came from the Messenger (صَلَّى اللَّهُ عَلَيْهِ وَسَلَّمَ). As for the fact that some people did not come across it, did not know about it, or did not want to know about it is not proof, because total-clarification has taken place. How could it be the case that the Messenger clarified to his *Ummah* everything, even the etiquettes of using the bathroom, but did not clarify to them the ʿ*aqīdah*, but these [*Khalaf*] came later on and explained it?" (p. 45-46)

[2] **(MA):** "The supreme good he knew for us was knowledge of Allāh, and he led us to knowing Him through His Names and Attributes. The worse of what he knew would harm us was being ignorant of Allāh, associating partners with Him, and taking on a methodology other than what he left us upon. The methodology [he left us upon] is manifested in his statement: 'I left you upon a clear white plain'... this is the methodology of the *Salaf al-Ṣāliḥ*. If you are asked what the methodology of the *Salaf al-Ṣāliḥ* is, then you say this is it; that white clear plain whose night is similar to its day (i.e. having no obscurity)." (1/44)

and those who forgot it did so." Reported by al-Bukhārī—so it is impossible, after him teaching them everything that would benefit them in the religion, even precise and subtle matters [like the etiquettes of using the bathroom], that he would leave off teaching them what to utter with their tongues and believe with their hearts concerning their Lord, the One whom they worship, Lord of all creation.[1] This is because awareness of Him is the pinnacle of knowledge, worshipping Him is the greatest objective, and reaching Him is the peak of what one desires. Rather, this is the essence of the Prophetic call and the main theme of the Divine Scripture.

So, how can one who has an inkling of faith and wisdom presume that the Messenger (ﷺ) did not clarify this subject in the best and most complete manner; and since this did occur, it would be impossible that the best of his *Ummah* and the best of its generations were careless regarding this subject, either adding to it, or taking away from it.[2] It is likewise impossible that the praiseworthy generations—the generation in which the Prophet was sent, then

---

[1] **(SF):** "The Shaykh is clarifying to them that it is impossible that the Messenger (ﷺ) did not explain this matter which is the foundation of the religion, and likewise it is impossible that the Companions remained silent about it and did not convey this clarification to the people. Therefore, the argument of the opposition revolves around one of two matters:

1- Either the Messenger concealed the truth and did not clarify it to the people, [and to say this] is disbelief because it is accusing the Messenger (ﷺ) [of that which he is innocent of].

2- Or he did clarify it, but the Companions concealed it and did not clarify it [to those after them], and this is accusing the Companions of concealing the truth and not conveying it to the people..." (p. 48)

[2] **(MA):** "It is impossible that any of this could have transpired from the [Companions]. Not because they are infallible, but because the Messenger of Allāh testified that they are the best of people. They did not become the best of people except through knowledge; complete knowledge of what the Messenger of Allāh came with, acting by it, and calling to it." (1/48)

those who followed them, then those who followed them—were not aware and did not profess the manifest truth in this subject, because the opposite of this would mean that they lacked this knowledge and did not speak on it, or they held a belief contrary to the truth and spoke with what opposes it, and both these scenarios are impossible as it relates to them.[1]

As for the first, anyone who has the least amount of life in their heart, or [desire] to seek knowledge or to worship, then investigating this subject, inquiring about it, and [wanting] to know the truth regarding it would be his greatest goal and ultimate objective. What I mean is clarification of the correct belief one must hold, [not meaning] seeking to know the exact nature (i.e. *al-kayfiyyah*) of the Lord and His Attributes. Pure souls desire nothing more than to have knowledge of this matter, as is known by way of the natural-disposition (*fiṭrah*) and one's instinct.[2] So, because this is [naturally]

---

[1] **(SF):** "[The claim] that the Companions and the *Tābiʿīn* did not know this subject raises two possibilities: Either they were ignorant, [which is impossible] because they were the most knowledgeable of generations after the Messenger (ﷺ), or either they concealed it. This would mean that they knew of it and did not clarify it, nor did they convey it to the people, nor did [the *Tābiʿīn*] convey to [the people] what reached them from the Companions of the Messenger of Allāh (ﷺ). These virtuous generations are innocent of both these claims." (p. 52)

[2] **(SF):** "The souls do not yearn for anything more than to know Allāh's Names, Attributes, His Oneness, and the correct creed which they must believe regarding their Lord (سُبْحَانَهُ وَتَعَالَىٰ), and knowing Allāh, His Greatness, His Majesty, and the worship that is due to Him alone. This is the greatest matter in which the soul finds pleasure, because if you know your Lord you will love Him, worship Him, and seek to draw near to Him. If you know His Greatness, His Ability, His Exaltedness, and His Mercy, and likewise His severe retribution and His anger, you will draw near to Him through what He loves and stay away from what He hates. So the souls do not yearn for anything more as they do for this. How can you worship your Lord without knowing Him by way of His Names and Attributes? Such a Lord will be unknown. However,

present [within those with pure souls]—which is considered from the strongest proofs—how can one imagine that this can be absent among those elite individuals during their generations as a whole?[1] This can almost never occur from the most dull-witted person and most obstinate one who turns away from Allāh, and the most eager of those who seek the worldly life, heedless of the remembrance of Allāh,[2] so how can it ever occur with them (i.e. the praiseworthy generations)?

---

if you know Him by way of His Names, Attributes, His signs, and His creation, it will show you His greatness and that He is deserving of all worship. If you were to look at the creation of the heavens and the earth and its wonders, you will say just as the believers say,

﴿رَبَّنَا مَا خَلَقْتَ هَٰذَا بَٰطِلًا سُبْحَٰنَكَ فَقِنَا عَذَابَ ٱلنَّارِ﴾

> **"Our Lord, you have not created all this without purpose, glory be to You! Give us salvation from the torment of the Fire."** [Sūrah Āl 'Imrān 3:191]

You will know Allāh and His greatness when you ponder over His creation. The one who is Able to create all of these remarkable, marvelous creations points to His Greatness, His Ability, His Knowledge, and Wisdom (سُبْحَانَهُ وَتَعَالَى). Therefore, you know your Lord by way of His signs and Attributes (سُبْحَانَهُ وَتَعَالَى). (p. 53)

[1] **(MA):** "[Meaning], the generation of the Companions, the *Tābi'īn*, and the generation after the *Tābi'īn*." (1/50)

[2] **(MA):** "No matter how dull-witted a person is, or obstinate, turning away from Allāh (سُبْحَانَهُ وَتَعَالَى), it is a must that they have some type of desire to know Allāh (سُبْحَانَهُ وَتَعَالَى) by His Names and Attributes. And no matter how eager a person is in seeking out the worldly affairs, this would not prevent him from learning something in this subject. Hence, those elite individuals (i.e. the Companions) whom have dedicated all their time in gaining knowledge of Allāh (سُبْحَانَهُ وَتَعَالَى) and knowing what the Messenger of Allāh (صَلَّى ٱللَّهُ عَلَيْهِ وَسَلَّمَ) came with, how can they be accused of deficiency in their knowledge of this matter?" (1/50)

And as for [the *Salaf*] holding a belief regarding [Allāh's Attributes] that contradicts the truth, or professing [other than it], then no Muslim or one with intellect who knew their condition would ever believe that. Further, their speech on this subject is too much to even possibly try to mention in this *Fatwā*, or in a larger work. Anyone who researches and looks into it would know this. Also, it is impossible that latecomers could be more knowledgeable than the early predecessors, as some fools who have not given the *Salaf* their due respect have stated: "The way of the *Salaf* is safer, while the way of the *Khalaf* is more knowledgeable and more precise."[1] But rather [it is they who] do not know Allāh, His Messenger, and those who believe in Him with the true required knowledge.

These innovators who prefer the way of the *Khalaf* over the way of the *Salaf* were deluded due to believing that the way of the *Salaf* is merely belief in the wordings of the *Qur'ān* and *Ḥadīth* without understanding. Just like the illiterate people whom Allāh said regarding,

﴿ وَمِنْهُمْ أُمِّيُّونَ لَا يَعْلَمُونَ ٱلْكِتَٰبَ إِلَّآ أَمَانِيَّ وَإِنْ هُمْ إِلَّا يَظُنُّونَ ﴿٧٨﴾ ﴾

[1] **(SF):** "The Shaykh is going to refute this statement, just as others have refuted it, because this [statement] is misguidance and ascribes misguidance and ignorance to the *Salaf*...due to their stupidity they say that the way of the *Salaf* is safer while the way of the *Khalaf* is more knowledgeable and more precise. This is contradiction. Safety does not come about except with knowledge, and there is no safety with ignorance. Further, could it be possible that the *Khalaf* be more knowledgeable than the *Salaf* who learned directly from the Messenger (صَلَّىٰ ٱللَّهُ عَلَيْهِ وَسَلَّمَ), and also from the Companions? Is it possible that the generations which came later be more knowledgeable than the *Salaf*, when the Prophet (صَلَّىٰ ٱللَّهُ عَلَيْهِ وَسَلَّمَ) said: 'The best of you are my generation, then those who follow them then those who follow them.'" (p. 56-57)

> **"And there are among the (Jews) illiterates who know not the Book, but they trust upon false desires."** [Sūrah *al-Baqarah* 2:78][1]

[And they believed] that the way of the *Khalaf* is extracting the understanding of the texts which are altered from their realities by using different types of metaphors (*majāzāt*) and uncommon lexical-terminologies.

Therefore, that corrupt belief—which entails throwing Islām behind one's back—is what brought about that [false] statement.[2] No doubt they have lied upon the way of the *Salaf* and are misguided in

---

[1] **(SF):** "Can these philosophers be compared to Abū Bakr, 'Umar, 'Uthmān, 'Alī, and the rest of the Companions, and the *Muhājirūn* and *Anṣār*? Can they be compared to the *Tābi'īn*, the followers of the *Tābi'īn*, and the praiseworthy generations, when their sole knowledge is that of philosophy, logic, and debate, which was taken from the Greek philosophers? The *Salaf* took [their knowledge] from the Messenger (ﷺ), and held on to the Book and *Sunnah*. How can one compare between those who took knowledge from the Book and *Sunnah* and those who only learned the sciences of philosophy, logic, debate, and speculative theology which was brought by the disbelieving Greek philosophers who were ignorant of the [Islāmic] legislation?" (p. 59)

[2] **(MA):** "If the *Salaf* did not understand the Book and the *Sunnah*, then from where did we understand it, and from where did the *Khalaf* understand it? These innovators have lied on the way of the *Salaf* by describing them as being simply those who read the text [without understanding], and they are also misguided due to ascribing correctness to the way of the *Khalaf* by claiming that it is more precise and more knowledgeable. Hence, they combined between being ignorant of the way of the *Salaf* by lying on them and claiming that they have the similitude of an illiterate people, and between foolishness and misguidance by ascribing correctness to the way of the *Khalaf*. Therefore, what is the correct way? The correct way is to believe that the *Salaf* of this *Ummah* were more knowledgeable, more precise, safer, and possessed more understanding than those who came after them. Furthermore, there is no safety for those who come after them unless they tread their path..." (1/56)

ascribing correctness to the way of the *Khalaf*. Thus, they have combined between being ignorant of the way of the *Salaf* by lying upon them, and between foolishness along with misguidance by ascribing correctness to the way of the *Khalaf*.[1]

And the reason behind this is their belief that these texts (i.e. the *Qur'ān* and *Sunnah*) do not point to [the reality] of any Attribute, based upon corrupt doubts which they share with their brethren from the disbelievers.[2] So because they believed [Allāh's] Attributes to be non-existent, along with the fact that these texts must carry a

---

[1] **(SF):** "They lied upon the *Salaf* by attributing ignorance to them and *tafwīḍ*, and they went astray by praising the way of the *Khalaf*, which is explaining the texts [of the Attributes] with other than their proper meanings. Therefore, they combined between lying upon the *Salaf*, and misguidance by giving preference to the *Khalaf*." (p. 61)

[2] **(MA):** "Who are their brethren from the disbelievers? The philosophers, because this *'aqīdah* was introduced to them by way of the philosophers. The philosophers are the teachers of the *Jahmiyyah* and *Mu'tazilah*..." (1/61)

(SF): "These are their doubts which led them astray:

The First Doubt: They thought that the *Salaf* did not comprehend the meanings of the texts.

The Second Doubt: They thought that Allāh did not possess Attributes, that these texts do not point to Allāh's Attributes, and that the [texts] should not be understood by their apparent meanings. Therefore, it was a must to reinterpret those texts and distort them from their apparent wordings, because [as they claim] they do not point to [true] Attributes. This is the reason for their misguidance...The reason for their misguidance was making *ta'ṭīl*—which means to reject and strip Allāh (سُبْحَانَهُ وَتَعَالَى) of all Attributes—due to them believing that Allāh did not have any [true] Attributes, and that He is a mere Essence that cannot be described with Attributes. However, because the texts are manifestly clear in affirming Attributes for Allāh, what could they do? It was not possible that they could reject the texts outright, so they resorted to distorting them [from their apparent meanings]. Instead of rejecting the texts, they distorted their meanings and twisted them in order to escape the first blunder that they fell into, but they inevitably fell into one greater than that." (p. 61-62)

meaning, they wavered between having belief (*īmān*) in the Attribute and [claiming to] entrust [the knowledge of its] meaning [to Allāh] (*tafwīḍ*)—which they [erroneously] claimed to be the way of the *Salaf*[1]—and between distorting the Attribute to other

---

[1] **(MA):** "The *Mu'awwilah* (i.e. those who distort Allāh's Attributes) all unite upon one factor when they distort [Allāh's Attributes]; meaning when they distort the text containing Attributes [of Allāh]; It is only one factor [they unite upon] nothing more, and that is [their claim that affirming these Attributes] is logically impossible. It is logically impossible that Allāh (سُبْحَانَهُ وَتَعَالَى) can be described with *Istiwā* (Rising) above His throne, *al-Nuzūl* (descending), *al-Majī'* (Coming forth), *al-Faraḥ* (Happiness), *al-Riḍā* (Being pleased), *al-Maḥabbah* (Love), and other *ṣifāt khabariyyah*. Their factor in uniting is one thing, which is that these texts are logically impossible. Therefore, [as they claim], if you come across any of these texts you must do one of two things: either you distort the meaning of [the Attribute] and say that this *ta'wīl* (distortion) is the way of the *Khalaf* -which they claimed to be more knowledgeable- or you make *tafwīḍ* of those texts by saying 'I do not know the meaning of *Istawā* (to rise), or *Nazala* (to descend), or *Jā'a*(to come).' Is it possible for an Arab to claim that he does not know the meaning of *Jā'a*, or *Atā* (i.e. to come), or *Istawā*? If so he is feigning ignorance; he is feigning to be ignorant of the meanings of these texts and thus claims to make *tafwīḍ* (entrusting) the knowledge of their meanings to Allāh. They call this absolute *tafwīḍ*, and this is incorrect. What is correct is that *tafwīḍ* is of two types:

(1) Absolute *tafwīḍ* as regards to the meanings, the how, and the reality [of these texts]. This is the way of the ignorant *Mufawwiḍah* and is not the way of the *Salaf*.

(2) Making *tafwīḍ* [i.e. entrusting] of the "how" (*al-kayfiyyah*) and the reality [of these texts to Allāh], while maintaining the fact that the [linguistic] meanings are known. So the general-meanings of the texts are known due to them being in the plain Arabic language. This is what Imām Mālik alluded to in his statement: '*Al-Istiwā* is known.' If the verb *Istawā* is used with the particle "*'alā*", it means highness (*al-'uluw*),

﴿ٱلرَّحْمَٰنُ عَلَى ٱلْعَرْشِ ٱسْتَوَىٰ﴾

"The Most Beneficent rose over (*Istawā*) the throne."

[meanings] using somewhat burdensome [methods], and this is what they call the way of the *Khalaf*.[1] As a result, this falsehood became a mixture of corrupt reasoning along with negation of the texts. This is because in their negation [of Allāh's Attributes] they relied upon intellectual-[arguments] which they thought to be manifest proofs, but in reality, were only doubts, and at the same time they distorted the verses of the [*Qur'ān*] from their proper context.

Hence, because they based their affair upon these two disbelieving premises,[2] the end result was ascribing ignorance and foolishness to

---

The meaning of the word *Istawā* is known. [Imām Mālik said,] 'and the *kayf* [i.e. how it occurs] is unknown.' How Allāh (سُبْحَانَهُ وَتَعَالَىٰ) rose above His throne is unknown to us, and out of the realms of our comprehension. 'Belief [*Imān*] in *al-Istiwā* is obligatory,' in order to deem truthful what Allāh informed of, 'And asking how *al-Istiwā* occurs is an innovation…' The point is, the *tafwīḍ* made by the *Salaf* is regarding the 'how' and reality [of the texts containing Allāh's Attributes], not *tafwīḍ* of their meanings and removing them from their apparent linguistic context…" (1/63)

[1] **(SF):** "Because they believed Allāh does not possess Attributes, although the *Qur'ān* and *Sunnah* has affirmed Attributes for Allāh in many verses - which is something they cannot deny - they broke down into two categories:
The First: Those who reinterpreted the meanings and distorted them. They are known as the *Mu'aṭṭilah*.
The Second: Those who stopped, and [claimed] to leave its knowledge to Allāh, and they are known as the *Mufawwiḍah*. They say: "We do not explain [the Attributes], rather we leave their explanation to Allāh. [They say], as for [the word itself], it does not point to an attribute, and we do not know its meaning. This is what they claimed to be the [the way of] the *Salaf*; that [the *Salaf*] affirmed the wordings but denied knowledge of their meanings. So they attributed their disease and sickness to the *Salaf*, however it is them who are truly *Mufawwiḍah*, not the *Salaf*." (p. 63)

[2] **(MA):** "[He called these disbelieving premises] because they are attributed and return back to the disbelievers; the chain of the *Jahmiyyah* goes back to the Jew

[the *Salaf*], and belief that they were an illiterate people; nothing more than righteous laymen[1] who had not gained deep insight into the realities of awareness of Allāh, and did not comprehend the intricacies of divine revelation. Rather, it was the "virtuous" *Khalaf* who obtained prominence in all of this.[2]

Further, if a person was to ponder over this statement, they would find that it is the pinnacle of ignorance—nay the pinnacle of misguidance. [3] How can these later generations [be more knowledgeable than the *Salaf*]—especially when those referred to here as "*Khalaf*" are a party of *Ahl al-Kalām* whom are confused in matters of the Religion and are blindfolded from having [true] knowledge of Allāh.

Labīd Ibn al-'Aṣam, the magician who placed magic on the Prophet (صَلَّى ٱللَّهُ عَلَيْهِ وَسَلَّمَ). Jahm took this *'aqīdah* from Ja'd Ibn Dirham, and Ja'd took it from those Jews whose leader was Labīd Ibn al-'Aṣam, the Jewish magician." (1/65)

[1] **(SF):** "They based their *madhhab* on two premises:

One: That the *Salaf* did not understand the *Qur'ān* whereas the *Khalaf* do.

Two: That the proofs of the *Qur'ān* and *Sunnah* are speculative, whereas the proofs of the [science of] logic are definitive. The result of these two premises which are based upon ascribing ignorance and heedlessness to the *Salaf* and deeming them as mere righteous laymen - at the same time ascribing intelligence to the *Khalaf* and giving them precedence in knowledge- the end result was that they deemed the *Salaf* to be ignorant and illiterate people who memorized but had no understanding. They merely memorized words and were clueless of their meanings. (p. 64-65)

[2] **(MA):** "Here, [Shaykh al-Islām] mocks them [by calling them virtuous], and they are deserving of this sarcasm." (1/65)

[3] **(SF):** "If we abandon the *Salaf* and say that they were ignorant, or people who were heedless, not having any knowledge, then where will we take our religion from? From Jahm Ibn Ṣafwān, Wāṣil Ibn 'Aṭā, et al.? If we were to leave off Abū Bakr, 'Umar, 'Uthmān, 'Alī and the Companions, and the *Tābi'īn*, do we then take knowledge from the *Jahmiyyah*, *Mu'tazilah* and their off shoots? This is the pinnacle of misguidance." (p. 65-66)

And one who observed the furthermost limits (of speculative theology) informed about the end point of the aspirations (of the theologians) when he said:

"Verily, I have travelled to all the institutions [of the logicians], and I moved about frequently among those places. But I only saw people rubbing their chin in confusion or grinding their teeth out of regret."[1]

Rather some of them have acknowledged this against their own selves from their statements, citing others, or what they mentioned in their own authored works, such as the statement of one of their leaders:

---

[1] **(SF):** "This person went to all of their scholars and their schools seeking the truth, but did not attain it. Each of them pointed him to a different path. He found that some of them were either confused or regretful because they knew that they were misguided and became sorrowful. This is their outcome due to them not relying upon the Book of Allāh and *Sunnah* of the Messenger of Allāh (ﷺ), and upon the guidance of the pious predecessors, which direct to the correct path…" (p. 67)

(TN): These lines of poetry were mentioned by Abū ʿAbdullāh al-Shahrastānī in the beginning of his book "*Nihāyah al-Iqdām Fī ʿIlm al-Kalām*" without being attributed to anyone, and some scholars have attributed these lines to al-Shahrastānī himself.

And how excellent is the reply of al-Amīr al-Ṣanʿānī to those lines of poetry, when he said:

لَعَلَّكَ أهْمَلْتَ الطَّوافَ بِمَعْهَدِ　　　الرَّسولِ ومَنْ لاقاهُ مِنْ كُلِّ عالِمِ

فَما حارَ مَنْ يَهْدِي بِهَدِي مُحَمّدٍ　　　ولَسْتَ تَراهُ قارِعاً سِنَّ نادِمِ

"Perhaps you were heedless in visiting the learning place of the Messenger, and that of the scholars who met him (i.e. the Companions). No one who sought guidance with the guidance of Muḥammad has become confused, nor do you see them grinding their teeth in regret."

"The end result of pushing the intellect [past it limits] is deadlock,[1] and most striving done by [the logicians] is misguidance. Our souls within our bodies have feelings of loneliness,[2] and the result of our worldly life is only harm and evil consequence. Throughout our lifetime we have not benefitted from our research, except gathering hearsay.[3] I have pondered over the methods of speculative theology and that of the philosophers, and I found that they do not amount to any benefit whatsoever. And I found that the soundest way is the way of the *Qur'ān*. I read in affirmation,

﴿ٱلرَّحۡمَٰنُ عَلَى ٱلۡعَرۡشِ ٱسۡتَوَىٰ﴾

> **"The Most Beneficent rose over (*Istawā*) the throne,"**

And,

﴿إِلَيۡهِ يَصۡعَدُ ٱلۡكَلِمُ ٱلطَّيِّبُ﴾

---

[1] **(MA):** "No matter how much the intellect seeks advancement, especially as it relates to studies concerning the Lord (i.e. His Essence, Names and Attributes, Actions etc.) the end result will be deadlock, [as the intellect has limits]." (1/71)

[2] **(MA):** "Their souls lacked nourishment, and the nourishment of the souls is revelation; the Speech of Allāh, and the remembrance of Allāh. They turned away from Allāh, His Speech, and what His Messenger came with, thus they became in a state of separation and loneliness." (1/71)

[3] **(MA):** "Aristotle said this, Ibn Sīnā said that, al-Fārābī said this; [i.e. the top logicians]. They were not given success to say Allāh said and His Messenger said (صَلَّى ٱللَّهُ عَلَيْهِ وَسَلَّمَ)…" (1/72)

(SF): "This statement is from one of their leaders, Abū 'Abdullāh al-Rāzī, author of the *Tafsīr*. He repented to Allāh (عَزَّوَجَلَّ) at the end of his life, as he mentioned in these lines of poetry." (p. 68)

"To Him ascends all good words."
[Sūrah al-Fāṭir 35:10]

And I read in negation,

﴿لَيْسَ كَمِثْلِهِۦ شَىْءٌ وَهُوَ ٱلسَّمِيعُ ٱلْبَصِيرُ﴾

"There is nothing similar to Him and He is All-Hearer, All Seer," [Sūrah al-Shūrā 42:11]

[And,]

﴿وَلَا يُحِيطُونَ بِهِۦ عِلْمًا﴾

"They will never encompass anything of His knowledge." [Sūrah Tā Hā 20:110]

So, whoever experienced the things that I have, will know exactly as I have come to know."[1]

Another from among them stated: "I have entered the vast ocean [of speculative theology], and left off the people of Islām and their knowledge.[2] I've indulged in what [the Scholars] have forbade me from,[3] and now if my Lord does not grant me His Mercy, then woe

[1] **(SF):** "This is a testimony in favor of the people of the *Sunnah*. This person did not find a safer and more righteous path than theirs, nor [a way] more correct than using the *Qur'ān* as evidence…" (p. 69)

[2] **(MA):** "The sciences of the people of Islām is that which is taken from the *Qur'ān* and *Sunnah*." (1/73)

[3] **(MA):** "Meaning, speculative theology." (1/74)

to *fulān* (i.e. himself). And here I am, dying upon the *'aqīdah* of my mother."[1]

Also, another one stated, "Those having the most doubt at the time of death are the people of speculative theology."[2]

---

[1] **(MA):** "What was the *'aqīdah* of his mother? It was the *fiṭrah* [natural-disposition to believe in Allāh and His Highness above His creation]. After all this rhetoric, he returned to the *'aqīdah* of an old woman. The *'aqīdah* of the *fiṭrah* which the slave girl was upon, who some latecomers tried to defame and claim she was unstable. The slave girl whom the Messenger of Allāh (ﷺ) asked, 'Where is Allāh?' She replied, 'Above the heavens.' He then asked her, 'Who am I?' She replied, 'You are the Messenger of Allāh (ﷺ).' So the [the Prophet's] response was, 'Free her for indeed she is a believer (*Mu'minah*).' This [*'aqīdah*] is the *'aqīdah* of old women [from the Muslims], likewise the *'aqīdah* of the mother of al-Juwaynī which he stated he was dying upon and abandoning speculative rhetoric. All of this transpired after the people of his land named him '*Imām al-Ḥaramayn*' (i.e. Imām of the two holy precincts, Makkah and al-Madinah), although he never once led a prayer in either *masjid*..." (1/74)

(SF): "These words are attributed to Abū al-Ma'ālī al-Juwaynī who was from their Imāms and prominent figures...he went with *Ahl al-Kalām* and wasted his entire life in the science of theological-debate and did not seek understanding of the Book and *Sunnah*, although the *Salaf* had forewarned about speculative theology and debate. They said it does not lead to anything except confusion and incertitude. So, this is what al-Juwaynī said at his time of death, and this is his recanting and his acknowledgement that these paths are erroneous." (p. 70)

[2] **(SF):** "This is one of their testimonies regarding the falsehood of the way of the logicians. They have doubt in their *'aqīdah* at the time of death because they never learned what will cause them to be saved when it approaches." (p. 70)

(TN): This statement is attributed to Abū Ḥāmid al-Ghazālī. Shaykh al-Islām Ibn Taymiyyah stated, "Their leaders do not cease to inform that their way is lacking proofs and guidance, as we mentioned about the statement of Abū Ḥāmid and others. To the extent Abū Ḥāmid al-Ghazālī said, 'Those having the most doubt at the time of death are the people of speculative theology.'" See *Majmū' al-Fatāwā* (4/24).

Moreover, these logicians who oppose the *Salaf*, if they are investigated [and tested,][1] [you would not find] with them any true knowledge of Allāh or factual-awareness of Him. They cannot comprehend it if was in front of them, nor would they realize it after it has passed them[2]. So how can these blinded, deficient, reckless, confused, latecomers be more knowledgeable about Allāh and His Names and Attributes, and more precise concerning His verses and His Essence, than the foremost [to embrace Islām] from the *Muhājirūn*, the *Anṣār*, and those who followed them in goodness, from the heirs of the Prophets and successors of the Messengers; the signposts of guidance, and the guiding lamps [through] darkness. Those who recited, implemented, and spread the Book (i.e. *Qur'ān*), and because of it they were granted aid and victory; [those] whom the Book spoke of [in praise] and they spoke with the Book; those whom Allāh granted knowledge and wisdom to the extent they stood out over the rest of the followers of the Prophets, let alone the rest of the nations who have no book. They possessed the most sound, deep, and precise knowledge, to the point if the philosophies of every [nation] besides them were gathered next to [theirs], one would be shy to attempt to make a comparison.

Furthermore, how can the best of generations (i.e. the *Salaf*) be less in knowledge and wisdom than these youths—in comparison to

---

[1] **(MA):** "If they were to be tested regarding what they studied or learned regarding knowledge of Allāh, or what relates to the Prophets, or the affairs of the unseen such as matters of the Hereafter..." (1/77)

[2] **(MA):** "Meaning, they have nothing whatsoever, rather they are ignoramuses. For this reason, if Shaykh al-Islām would debate them and they would remain persistent upon their beliefs, he would say to them: 'If I was in your place, I would have ruled myself to be a disbeliever, however you all are ignoramuses,' although they saw themselves to be the most knowledgeable of people..." (1/77-78)

them—especially relating to knowledge of Allāh and the rulings regarding His verses and Names? Or how can the descendants of the philosophers and the followers of [the people] of Hind and the Greeks and their heirs from the Magians, polytheists, and the misguided Jews, Christians, and Sabians and those similar to them, be more knowledgeable than the heirs of the Prophets and the people of *Qur'ān* and *īmān* (faith)?[1]

Hence, I only began with this introduction, because the one who has it firmly established will know where true guidance lies in this subject[2] and other than it. Just as one will know that misguidance and confusion have only prevailed over many of the latecomers due to them tossing the Book of Allāh behind their backs[3] and turning away from the clear evidences and guidance that Allāh sent Muḥammad (صَلَّىٰ ٱللَّٰهُ عَلَيْهِ وَسَلَّمَ) with. Also, them leaving off searching for the path of the early predecessors and *Tābi'īn*, and [instead] seeking knowledge of Allāh from those who did not know Him based upon their own acknowledgement, the testimony of the *Ummah*, and countless other proofs.[4] Further, my objective is not [to discuss] one [person in particular], however I will give descriptions of each accordingly...

End of Introduction to *al-Fatwā al-Ḥamawiyyah*

---

[1] **(MA):** "Meaning this can never be the case. He presented a rhetorical-question meant to rebuke them..." (1/79)

[2] **(MA):** "As it relates to Allāh's Names and Attributes, and other areas [of knowledge]." (1/84)

[3] **(MA):** "Whereas they did not seek guidance from the Book of Allāh, but rather sought guidance from other than the Book of Allāh, so Allāh led them astray." (1/84)

[4] **(MA):** "They have ruled upon their own selves as being ignorant, so how can knowledge be sought from their likes? From the books of al-Rāzī, al-Shahrastānī, al-Ghazālī, al-Juwaynī, when they all have ruled upon themselves as being ignorant and having regret for what they indulged in..." (1/86)

The English Text of the Introduction to al-Fatwā al-Ḥamawiyyah Without Commentary

In the year 698H, the great scholar Shaykh al-Islām Taqī al-Dīn Abū al-ʿAbbās Aḥmad Ibn ʿAbd al-Ḥalīm Ibn ʿAbd al-Salām Ibn Taymiyyah was asked [this question], and because of [his] answer, matters [of hearings, judgments] and tribulations transpired. It is an answer containing tremendous benefit.

The questioner asked:

What is the statement of the pre-eminent Scholars, the Imams of the Religion, regarding the verses containing the Attributes (*ṣifāt*) [of Allāh], such as His statement (عَزَّوَجَلَّ),

﴿ٱلرَّحْمَٰنُ عَلَى ٱلْعَرْشِ ٱسْتَوَىٰ ﴿٥﴾﴾

"The Most Beneficent (Allāh) **rose over** (*Istawā*) **the throne."** [Sūrah Tā Hā 20:5]

And His statement (عَزَّوَجَلَّ),

﴿ثُمَّ ٱسْتَوَىٰٓ إِلَى ٱلسَّمَآءِ وَهِىَ دُخَانٌ﴾

"Then He rose over (*Istawā*) **towards the heavens when it was smoke."**

[Sūrah al-Fuṣṣilat 41:11]

And other verses and *aḥādīth* containing [His] Attributes, such as his saying (ﷺ), "Verily the hearts of the children of Ādam are between two Fingers from the Fingers of the Most Merciful,[1]" and his saying, "*al-Jabbār* [i.e. Allāh] will place His Foot in the Hell-Fire..."[2] and similar *aḥādith* [of this sort], and what do the scholars say [regarding them]? [Please] give a detailed answer regarding that, and may you be rewarded, if Allāh wills.

[Shaykh al-Islām] answered:

All praise is due to Allāh, Lord of all creation. Our statement regarding [those texts containing Allāh's Attributes] is what Allāh and His Messenger have stated, as well as what was stated by the early Muslims who embraced Islām from the *Muhājirūn*, the *Anṣār*, and those who followed them in goodness, and the rightly guided Imāms after them; those whom the Muslims agree were rightly guided and possessed correct understanding. This is what is incumbent upon all people as it relates to this subject and other than it.

Indeed, Allāh sent Muḥammad (ﷺ) with guidance and the true Religion, in order to remove mankind from [layers of] darkness into light, by the permission of their Lord, to the path of the All-Mighty, One Full of Praise. [Allāh] testified that He sent him as a caller to [his Lord] by His permission, and [sent him] as an illuminating lamp. He commanded him to say,

---

[1] Reported by Muslim no. 2654 from the *ḥadīth* of ʿAbdullāh Ibn ʿAmr Ibn al-ʿAṣ (رَضِيَ ٱللَّهُ عَنْهُمَا).

[2] Reported by Bukhārī with a similar wording (no. 4849), and Muslim (no. 2848), from the *ḥadīth* of Abū Hurayrah (رَضِيَ ٱللَّهُ عَنْهُ).

﴿ قُلْ هَٰذِهِۦ سَبِيلِيٓ أَدْعُوٓاْ إِلَى ٱللَّهِۚ عَلَىٰ بَصِيرَةٍ أَنَا۠ وَمَنِ ٱتَّبَعَنِيۖ ﴾

"This is my path. I call to Allāh upon certain knowledge, I and whosoever follows me."

[Sūrah Yūsuf 12:108]

Therefore, it is impossible intellectually and religiously that this illuminating lamp (i.e. Muḥammad) whom Allāh sent in order to remove the people from [layers of] darkness into light, and revealed to him the Book (i.e. *Qur'ān*) in order to judge between the people in which they differ, just as He commanded the people to return disputes in their religion back to the Book and Wisdom (*ḥikmah*) which he was sent with, along with [the Prophet] calling to Allāh and to His path upon certain knowledge, by [Allāh's] permission, and He informed that He completed for him and his *Ummah* their religion, and perfected His favor upon them; it is impossible alongside this and other [considerations] that [the Prophet (صَلَّى ٱللَّهُ عَلَيْهِ وَسَلَّمَ)] left the subject of belief in Allāh and of knowledge regarding Him confusing and ambiguous, not having distinguished between what is incumbent for Allāh of beautiful Names and lofty Attributes, what is permitted for Him [of actions], and what is impossible for Him.

Surely, knowledge of [these matters] is the foundation of the religion and the basis of guidance. It is also the best thing the hearts can acquire, what the souls can achieve, and what the intellects can comprehend. Therefore, how can that Book (i.e. *Qur'ān*), that Messenger (i.e. Muḥammad), and the best of mankind after the Prophets (i.e. the Companions) not completely master this subject in respect to belief and statement? It is also impossible that the Prophet (صَلَّى ٱللَّهُ عَلَيْهِ وَسَلَّمَ) taught his *Ummah* everything, even the etiquettes of cleaning themselves [after using the bathroom][1]—and said: "I have left you upon a clear white plain, its night is like its day, no one strays from it except that he is destroyed."[2] There occurs in another authentic report, "Allāh never sent a Messenger except it was a duty upon him to point his *Ummah* to every good that he knew for them, and to warn them from every evil that he knew would harm them."[3] And Abū Dharr (رَضِيَ ٱللَّهُ عَنْهُ) said, "The Messenger of Allāh (صَلَّى ٱللَّهُ عَلَيْهِ وَسَلَّمَ) passed away, and there was not even a bird who flaps its wings in the sky except that he mentioned to us some knowledge concerning it."[4] And ʿUmar Ibn al-Khaṭṭāb (رَضِيَ ٱللَّهُ عَنْهُ) said: "The Messenger of Allāh (صَلَّى ٱللَّهُ عَلَيْهِ وَسَلَّمَ) stood among us [one day] and mentioned the matters of the very beginning of creation all the way until the people of Paradise enter their dwellings, and the people of the Hell-Fire enter their dwellings. Those who memorized it did so, and those who forgot it did so." Reported by al-Bukhārī[5]—so it is impossible, after him teaching them everything that would benefit them in the religion, even precise and subtle matters [like the etiquettes of using the bathroom], that he would leave off teaching them what to utter with their tongues and believe with their hearts concerning their Lord, the One whom they worship, Lord of all creation. This is because awareness of Him is the pinnacle of knowledge, worshipping Him is the greatest objective, and reaching

---

[1] Reported by Muslim (no. 262) from the *ḥādīth* of Salmān al-Fārisī (رَضِيَ ٱللَّهُ عَنْهُ).

[2] Reported by Ibn Mājah (no. 43), Aḥmad in his *Musnad*, Ibn Abū ʿĀṣim in his *Sunnah* (1/27) and declared *Ṣaḥīḥ* by Shaykh al-Albānī. See *al-Ṣaḥīḥah* (2/647, no. 937) from the *ḥādīth* of al-ʿIrbāḍ Ibn Sāriyah (رَضِيَ ٱللَّهُ عَنْهُ).

[3] Reported by Muslim (no. 1844) from the *ḥādīth* of ʿAbdullāh Ibn ʿAmr Ibn al-ʿAṣ (رَضِيَ ٱللَّهُ عَنْهُمَا).

[4] Reported by Aḥmad (5/153, 162) and declared *Ṣaḥīḥ* by Shaykh al-Albānī in *al-Ṣaḥīḥah* (no. 1803).

[5] (no. 3192)

Him is the peak of what one desires. Rather, this is the essence of the Prophetic call and the main theme of the Divine Scripture.

So, how can one who has an inkling of faith and wisdom presume that the Messenger (ﷺ) did not clarify this subject in the best and most complete manner; and since this did occur, it would be impossible that the best of his *Ummah* and the best of its generations were careless regarding this subject, either adding to it, or taking away from it. It is likewise impossible that the praiseworthy generations—the generation in which the Prophet was sent, then those who followed them, then those who followed them—were not aware and did not profess the manifest truth in this subject, because the opposite of this would mean that they lacked this knowledge and did not speak on it , or they held a belief contrary to the truth and spoke with what opposes it, and both these scenarios are impossible as it relates to them.

As for the first, anyone who has the least amount of life in their heart, or [desire] to seek knowledge or to worship, then investigating this subject, inquiring about it, and [wanting] to know the truth regarding it would be his greatest goal and ultimate objective. What I mean is clarification of the correct belief one must hold, [not meaning] seeking to know the exact nature (i.e. *al-kayfiyyah*) of the Lord and His Attributes. Pure souls desire nothing more than to have knowledge of this matter, as is known by way of the natural-disposition (*fiṭrah*) and one's instinct. So, because this is [naturally] present [within those with pure souls]—which is considered from the strongest proofs—how can one imagine that this can be absent among those elite individuals during their generations as a whole? This can almost never occur from the most dull-witted person and most obstinate one who turns away from Allāh, and the most eager of those who seek the worldly life, heedless of the remembrance of

Allāh, so how can it ever occur with them (i.e. the praiseworthy generations)?

And as for [the *Salaf*] holding a belief regarding [Allāh's Attributes] that contradicts the truth, or professing [other than it], then no Muslim or one with intellect who knew their condition would ever believe that. Further, their speech on this subject is too much to even possibly try to mention in this *Fatwā*, or in a larger work. Anyone who researches and looks into it would know this. Also, it is impossible that latecomers could be more knowledgeable than the early predecessors, as some fools who have not given the *Salaf* their due respect have stated: "The way of the *Salaf* is safer, while the way of the *Khalaf* is more knowledgeable and more precise." But rather [it is they who] do not know Allāh, His Messenger, and those who believe in Him with the true required knowledge.

These innovators who prefer the way of the *Khalaf* over the way of the *Salaf* were deluded due to believing that the way of the *Salaf* is merely belief in the wordings of the *Qur'ān* and *Ḥadīth* without understanding. Just like the illiterate people whom Allāh said regarding:

﴿ وَمِنْهُمْ أُمِّيُّونَ لَا يَعْلَمُونَ ٱلْكِتَٰبَ
إِلَّآ أَمَانِيَّ وَإِنْ هُمْ إِلَّا يَظُنُّونَ ٧٨ ﴾

> **"And there are among the (Jews) illiterates who know not the Book, but they trust upon false desires."** [Sūrah *al-Baqarah* 2:78]

[And they believed] that the way of the *Khalaf* is extracting the understanding of the texts which are altered from their realities by using different types of metaphors (*majāzāt*) and uncommon lexical-terminologies.

Therefore, that corrupt belief—which entails throwing Islām behind one's back—is what brought about that [false] statement. No doubt they have lied upon the way of the *Salaf* and are misguided in ascribing correctness to the way of the *Khalaf*. Thus, they have combined between being ignorant of the way of the *Salaf* by lying upon them, and between foolishness along with misguidance by ascribing correctness to the way of the *Khalaf*.

And the reason behind this is their belief that these texts (i.e. the *Qur'ān* and *Sunnah*) do not point to [the reality] of any Attribute, based upon corrupt doubts which they share with their brethren from the disbelievers. So because they believed [Allāh's] Attributes to be non-existent, along with the fact that these texts must carry a meaning, they wavered between having belief (*īmān*) in the Attribute and [claiming to] entrust [the knowledge of its] meaning [to Allāh] (*tafwīḍ*)—which they [erroneously] claimed to be the way of the *Salaf*—and between distorting the Attribute to other [meanings] using somewhat burdensome [methods], and this is what they call the way of the *Khalaf*. As a result, this falsehood became a mixture of corrupt reasoning along with negation of the texts. This is because in their negation [of Allāh's Attributes] they relied upon intellectual-[arguments] which they thought to be manifest proofs, but in reality, were only doubts, and at the same time they distorted the verses of the [*Qur'ān*] from their proper context.

Hence, because they based their affair upon these two disbelieving premises, the end result was ascribing ignorance and foolishness to [the *Salaf*], and belief that they were an illiterate people; nothing more than righteous laymen who had not gained deep insight into the realities of awareness of Allāh, and did not comprehend the intricacies of divine revelation. Rather it was the "virtuous" *Khalaf* who obtained prominence in all of this.

Further, if a person was to ponder over this statement, they would find that it is the pinnacle of ignorance—nay the pinnacle of misguidance. How can these later generations [be more knowledgeable than the *Salaf*]—especially when those referred to here as "*Khalaf*" are a party of *Ahl al-Kalām* whom are confused in matters of the religion and are blindfolded from having [true] knowledge of Allāh.

And one who observed the furthermost limits (of speculative theology) informed about the end point of the aspirations (of the theologians) when he said:

"Verily I have travelled to all the institutions [of the logicians], and I moved about frequently among those places. But I only saw people rubbing their chin in confusion or grinding their teeth out of regret."

Rather, some of them have acknowledged this against their own selves from their statements, citing others, or what they mentioned in their own authored works, such as the statement of one of their leaders:

"The end result of pushing the intellect [past it limits] is deadlock, and most striving done by [the logicians] is misguidance. Our souls within our bodies have feelings of loneliness, and the result of our worldly life is only harm and evil consequence. Throughout our lifetime we have not benefitted from our research, except gathering hearsay. I have pondered over the methods of speculative theology and that of the philosophers, and I found that they do not amount to any benefit whatsoever. And I found that the soundest way is the way of the *Qur'ān*. I read in affirmation,

﴿ٱلرَّحْمَٰنُ عَلَى ٱلْعَرْشِ ٱسْتَوَىٰ ۝٥﴾

"The Most Beneficent rose over (*Istawā*) the Throne."

And,

﴿إِلَيْهِ يَصْعَدُ ٱلْكَلِمُ ٱلطَّيِّبُ﴾

"To Him ascends all good words."
[Sūrah al-Fāṭir 35:10]

And I read in negation,

﴿لَيْسَ كَمِثْلِهِۦ شَىْءٌ ۖ وَهُوَ ٱلسَّمِيعُ ٱلْبَصِيرُ﴾

"There is nothing similar to Him and He is All-Hearer, All Seer." [Sūrah al-Shūrā 42:11]

[And],

﴿وَلَا يُحِيطُونَ بِهِۦ عِلْمًا﴾

"They will never encompass anything of His knowledge." [Sūrah Tā Hā 20:110]

So, whoever experienced the things that I have, will know exactly as I have come to know."

Another from among them stated, "I have entered the vast ocean [of speculative theology], and left off the people of Islām and their knowledge. I've indulged in what [the Scholars] have forbade me from, and now if my Lord does not grant me His Mercy, then woe to *fulān* (i.e. himself). And here I am, dying upon the *'aqīdah* of my mother."

Also, another one stated, "Those having the most doubt at the time of death are the people of speculative theology."

Moreover, these logicians who oppose the *Salaf*, if they are investigated [and tested], [you would not find] with them any true knowledge of Allāh or factual-awareness of Him. They cannot comprehend it if was in front of them, nor would they realize it after it has passed them. So how can these blinded, deficient, reckless, confused, latecomers be more knowledgeable about Allāh and His Names and Attributes, and more precise concerning His verses and His Essence, than the foremost [to embrace Islām] from the *Muhājirūn*, the *Anṣār*, and those who followed them in goodness, from the heirs of the Prophets and successors of the Messengers; the signposts of guidance, and the guiding lamps [through] darkness. Those who recited, implemented, and spread the Book (i.e. *Qur'ān*), and because of it they were granted aid and victory; [those] whom the Book spoke of [in praise] and they spoke with the Book; those whom Allāh granted knowledge and wisdom to the extent they stood out over the rest of the followers of the Prophets, let alone the rest of the nations who have no book. They possessed the most sound, deep, and precise knowledge, to the point if the philosophies of every [nation] besides them were gathered next to [theirs], one would be shy to attempt to make a comparison.

Furthermore, how can the best of generations (i.e. the *Salaf*) be less in knowledge and wisdom than these youths—in comparison to them—especially relating to knowledge of Allāh and the rulings regarding His verses and Names? Or how can the descendants of the philosophers and the followers of [the people] of Hind and the Greeks and their heirs from the Magians, polytheists, and the misguided Jews, Christians, and Sabians and those similar to them, be more knowledgeable than the heirs of the Prophets and the people of *Qur'ān* and *īmān* (faith)?

Hence, I only began with this introduction because the one who has it firmly established will know where true guidance lies in this subject and other than it. Just as one will know that misguidance and confusion have only prevailed over many of the latecomers due to them tossing the Book of Allāh behind their backs and turning away from the clear evidences and guidance that Allāh sent Muḥammad (صَلَّى ٱللَّهُ عَلَيْهِ وَسَلَّمَ) with. Also, them leaving off searching for the path of the early predecessors and *Tābi'īn*, and [instead] seeking knowledge of Allāh from those who did not know Him based upon their own acknowledgement, the testimony of the *Ummah*, and countless other proofs. Further, my objective is not [to discuss] one [person in particular], however I will give descriptions of each accordingly...

End of Introduction to *al-Fatwā al-Ḥamawiyyah*

◈◈◈

Summary of What is Entailed in the Introduction of al-Fatwā al-Ḥamawiyyah[1]

1- Allāh has completed the religion [of Islām] and perfected His favor upon the Messenger (صَلَّىٰ ٱللَّٰهُ عَلَيْهِ وَسَلَّمَ) and upon his *Ummah.*

2- The Prophet (صَلَّىٰ ٱللَّٰهُ عَلَيْهِ وَسَلَّمَ) left his *Ummah* upon a clear white plain, its night is like its day.

3- The methodology of the Prophet (صَلَّىٰ ٱللَّٰهُ عَلَيْهِ وَسَلَّمَ) in calling to the religion and belief, is that he called to Allāh upon clarity, knowledge, guidance, and a light from Allāh.

4- The Prophet (صَلَّىٰ ٱللَّٰهُ عَلَيْهِ وَسَلَّمَ) was the most aware of mankind concerning his Lord, and the most knowledgeable of them regarding His religion. Therefore, he was the most knowledgeable of mankind regarding his Lord, and possessed the most awe, and fear of Him. Additionally, he was one who was merciful to the believers.

5- The Messenger (صَلَّىٰ ٱللَّٰهُ عَلَيْهِ وَسَلَّمَ) taught his *ummah* matters of belief (*i'tiqād*) in specific, and matters of the religion in general; even the etiquettes of relieving one's self. Therefore, it is impossible that the Messenger (صَلَّىٰ ٱللَّٰهُ عَلَيْهِ وَسَلَّمَ) left his *Ummah* without teaching them [all] the affairs of their religion.

6- The Messenger (صَلَّىٰ ٱللَّٰهُ عَلَيْهِ وَسَلَّمَ) conveyed what was entrusted to him in a clear, complete fashion. Therefore, it is impossible that he could have left his *Ummah* in a state of confusion as it relates to belief [in Allah], and especially regarding [His] Attributes.

---

[1] *Al-Tuḥfah al-Siniyyah fī Bayān Maqāṣid al-Fatwā al-Ḥamawiyyah* (p. 109-110).

7- The testimony of the Companions (رَضِيَ ٱللَّهُ عَنْهُمْ) that the Messenger of Allāh (صَلَّى ٱللَّهُ عَلَيْهِ وَسَلَّمَ) taught them the affairs of their religion, and did not leave anything that the people were in need of except that he clarified it to them.

8- The obligation of following the Messenger (صَلَّى ٱللَّهُ عَلَيْهِ وَسَلَّمَ) and accepting *everything* that he came with.

9- In times of dispute between the *Ummah* of the Prophet (صَلَّى ٱللَّهُ عَلَيْهِ وَسَلَّمَ), it is a must to return [that differing] back to the Book of Allāh and to the *Sunnah* of the Prophet (صَلَّى ٱللَّهُ عَلَيْهِ وَسَلَّمَ) and his legislation, as the Messenger (صَلَّى ٱللَّهُ عَلَيْهِ وَسَلَّمَ) judged between the people in that which they differed.

10- The Companions (رَضِيَ ٱللَّهُ عَنْهُمْ) were upon the straight path in matters of the religion in general, and in the subject of belief (*iʿtiqād*) in specific. Therefore, it is impossible that the Companions and those who followed them in goodness were ignorant concerning the matter of belief [in Allāh and His Names and Attributes.]

11- The Companions (رَضِيَ ٱللَّهُ عَنْهُمْ) were the most knowledgeable of the people regarding Allāh and His Names and Attributes. They were not a people who spoke with falsehood, because speaking with falsehood occurs due to two reasons: a) Being ignorant of the truth. b) Wanting to mislead the people, and both of these possibilities are false as it relates to the Companions (رَضِيَ ٱللَّهُ عَنْهُمْ). Furthermore, they were not silent about the truth because remaining silent occurs due to two reasons: a) Being ignorant of the truth. b) Wanting to conceal knowledge, and both of these possibilities are false as it relates to the Companions (رَضِيَ ٱللَّهُ عَنْهُمْ). Therefore, the only possibilities left is that they were those who spoke with the truth and were the most knowledgeable of people concerning it.

The Arabic text of al-Fatwā al-Ḥamawiyyah

بسم الله الرحمن الرحيم

سُئِلَ شَيْخُ الإسلامِ العالِمُ الرَبانيُّ تقيُ الدينِ أبو العبّاس أحْمدُ بْنُ عبدِ الحليمِ بنِ عبدِ السلامِ بنِ تيمية رَحِمَهُ اللهُ تعالى، وذَلِكَ في سنةِ ثمانٍ وتسعين وستمائةٍ، وجَرَى بِسَبِبِ هذا الجوابِ أمورٌ ومحنٌ، وهُوَ جَوابٌ عظيمُ النفعِ جداً، فقالَ السَّائِلُ:

ما قَوْلُ السادَةِ العلماءِ أَئِمَةِ الدّينِ في آياتِ الصِفاتِ كَقَوْلِهِ تَعالى : { الرّحمنُ على العرشِ استَوى } وقَوْلُهُ : { ثم استَوى على العَرْش } وقَوْلُهُ : { ثم استَوى إلى السماءِ وَهِيَ دُخانٌ } إلى غيرِ ذلك مِنْ آياتِ الصِّفاتِ وَ أحاديثِ الصِّفاتِ كَقَوْلِهِ : صلى الله عليه وسلم { إنَّ قُلُوْبَ بَني آدمَ بَيْنَ أُصْبُعَيْنِ مِنْ أَصابِعِ الرّحْمَنِ } وقولُهُ : { يَضَعُ الجبّارُ قَدَمَهُ في النّارِ } إلى غيرِ ذلك وما قالَتِ العلماءُ فِيهِ وابْسَطُوا القولَ في ذلك مَأْجُوْرينَ إنْ شاء اللهُ تعالى .

فَأَجابَ:

الحمدُ للهِ ربِّ العالمينَ. قَوْلُنا فيها ما قالَهُ اللهُ ورَسولُهُ صلى الله عليه وسلم والسَّابِقُونَ الأَوَّلُونَ : مِنَ المهاجِرينَ وَالأَنْصارِ والذينَ اتَّبَعوهُمْ بإحْسانٍ ; وما قالهُ أَئِمَّةُ الهُدَى بَعْدَ هؤلاءِ الذين أجْمَعَ المسلمونَ على هِدايَتِهِمْ ودِرايَتِهِمْ وهذا هو الواجِبُ على جَميعِ الخَلْقِ في هذا البابِ وغَيْرِهِ ; فإنَّ اللهَ سُبحانَهُ وتعالى بَعَثَ محمداً صلى الله عليه وسلم بالهُدى ودينِ الحقِّ ; لِيُخْرِجَ الناسَ مِنَ الظُّلماتِ إلى النُّورِ بإذْنِ رَبِّهِمْ إلى صِراطِ العزيزِ الحميدِ وشَهِدَ لَهُ بأنَّهُ بَعَثَهُ داعِياً إلَيْهِ بإذْنِهِ وسِراجاً مُنيراً وأَمَرَهُ أنْ يَقُولَ : { قُلْ هذه سبيلي أدْعُو إلى اللهِ على بَصِيرةٍ أنا ومَنِ اتَّبعَنِي } .

فَمِنَ المُحالِ في العَقْلِ والدينِ أنْ يَكونَ السِّراجُ المنيرُ الذي أخْرَجَ اللهُ بِهِ النّاسَ مِنَ الظلماتِ إلى النورِ وأنْزَلَ مَعَهُ الكتابَ بالحقِّ لِيَحْكُمَ بينَ الناسِ فيما اخْتَلَفُوا فيهِ وأَمَرَ الناسَ أنْ يَرُدُّوا ما تنَازَعُوا فيهِ مِن أمْرِ دينِهِمْ إلى ما بُعِثَ به مِنَ الكتابِ والحِكْمَةِ وهُوَ يَدْعُو إلى اللهِ و إلى سَبيلِهِ بإذْنِهِ على بَصيرَةٍ و قَدْ أخْبَرَ اللهُ بأنه أكْمَلَ لَهُ ولأُمَّتِهِ دينَهُم وأتَمَّ عليهِمْ نِعْمَتَهُ - مُحالٌ مَعَ هذا وغَيرِهِ : أنْ يكونَ قَدْ تَرَكَ بابَ الإيمانِ باللهِ والعِلْمِ بهِ مُلْتَبِساً مُشْتَبِهًا فلَمْ يُمَيِّزْ بينَ ما يَجِبُ للهِ مِنَ الأسْماءِ الحُسْنى والصفاتِ العُليا وما يَجُوزُ عليه وما يَمْتَنِعُ عليه . فإنَّ مَعْرِفَةَ هذا أصلُ الدينِ وأساسُ الهِدايةِ

وأفْضَلُ وأوْجَبُ ما اكْتَسَبَتْهُ القُلُوبُ وحَصَّلَتْهُ النُّفُوسُ وأدْرَكَتْهُ العُقولُ فَكَيْفَ يكونُ ذلكَ الكتابُ وذلكَ الرَّسولُ وأفْضَلُ خَلْقِ اللهِ بعْدَ النَّبيينَ لمْ يُحْكِمُوا هذا البابَ اعْتِقاداً وقولاً ومِنَ المُحالِ أيضاً أنْ يكونَ النبيُّ صلى الله عليه وسلم قدْ عَلَّمَ أُمَّتَهُ كُلَ شيءٍ حتَّى الخِراءَةِ،

وقالَ صلى الله عليه وسلم:

{تَرَكْتُكُمْ على المَحَجَّةِ البَيْضاءِ لَيْلُها كَنهارِها لا يَزيغُ عَنْها بَعْدِي إلا هالِكٌ}

وقال فيما صحَّ عَنْهُ أيضاً: {ما بَعَثَ اللهُ مِن نبيٍّ إلا كانَ حقّاً عليه أنْ يَدُلَّ أُمَّتَهُ على خَيْرِ ما يَعلَمُهُ لَهُمْ ويَنْهاهُم عَنْ شَرِّ ما يَعْلَمُهُ لهمْ}.

وقال أبو ذَرٍّ: لَقَدْ تُوُفِّيَ رَسُولُ اللهُ صلى الله عليه وسلم وَمَا مِنْ طَائِرٍ يُقَلِّبُ جَنَاحَيْهِ فِي السَّمَاءِ إلا ذُكَرَ لَنَا مِنْهُ عِلْمًا.

وَقَالَ عُمَرُ بْنُ الخَطَّابِ: {قَامَ فِينا رَسُولُ اللهِ صلى الله عليه وسلم مُقَامًا فَذَكَرَ بَدءَ الخَلْقِ ; حَتَّى دَخَلَ أَهْلُ اَلجَنّةِ مَنَازِلَهُمْ وأَهْلُ النَّارِ مَنازِلَهُم حَفِظَ ذَلِكَ مَنْ حَفِظَهُ وَنَسِيهُ مَنْ نَسِيهُ} رَوَاهُ البُخاريُّ.

ومُحَالٌ مَعَ تَعْلِيمِهِمْ كُلَّ شَيْءٍ لَهُمْ فِيْهِ مَنْفَعةٌ فِي الدّينِ - وإِنْ دَقَّتْ - أَنْ يَتْرُكَ تَعْلِيمَهُمْ مَا يَقُولُونَهُ بِأَلْسِنَتِهِمْ وَيَعْتَقِدُونَهُ بِقُلُوبِهِمْ فِي رَبِّهِمِ وَمَعْبُودِهِمْ رَبِّ العَالَمِينَ الَّذِي مَعْرِفَتُهُ غَايَةُ اَلمعارِفِ وَعِبَادَتُهُ أَشْرَفُ اَلمَقَاصِدِ وَالْوُصُولُ إِلَيْهِ غَايَةُ اَلمطَالِبِ.

بَلْ هَذَا خُلاصَةُ الدَّعْوَةِ النَّبَوِيَّةِ وَزُبْدَةُ الرِّسَالَةِ الإِلَهِيَّةِ فَكَيْفَ يَتَوَهَّمُ مَنْ فِي قَلْبِهِ أَدْنَى مُسْكَةٍ مِنْ إِيمَانٍ وَحِكْمَةٍ أَنْ لاَ يَكُونَ بَيَانُ هَذاَ البَابِ قَدْ وَقَعَ مِنَ الرَّسُولِ عَلَى غَايَةِ التَّمَامِ ثُمَّ إِذَا كَانَ قَدْ وَقَعَ ذَلِكَ مِنْهُ: فَمِنَ المُحَالِ أَنْ يَكُونَ خَيْرُ أُمَّتِهِ وَأَفْضَلُ قُرُونِهَا قَصَّرُوا فِي هَذَا البَابِ زَائِدِينَ فِيهِ أَوْ نَاقِصِينَ عَنْهُ.

ثُمَّ مِنَ الْمُحَالِ أَيْضًا أَنْ تَكُونَ القُرُونُ الفَّاضِلَةُ - القَرْنُ الَّذِي بُعِثَ فِيهِمْ رَسُولُ الله صلى الله عليه وسلم ثُمَّ الَّذِينَ يَلُونَهُمْ ثُمَّ الَّذِينَ يَلُونَهُمْ - كَانُوا غَيْرَ عَالِمِينَ وَغَيْرَ قَائِلِينَ فِي هَذَا البَابِ بِالْحَقِّ المُبِينِ لأَنَّ ضِدَّ ذَلِكَ إِمَّا عَدَمُ العِلْمِ وَالْقَوْلِ وَإِمَّا اعْتِقَادُ نَقِيضِ الحَقِّ وَقَوْلُ خِلافِ الصِّدْقِ وَكِلاهُمَا مُمْتَنِعٌ.

أَمَّا الأَوَّلُ: فَلأَنَّ مَنْ فِي قَلْبِهِ أَدْنَى حَيَاةٍ وَطَلَبٍ لِلْعِلْمِ أَوْ نَهْمَةٍ فِي العِبَادَةِ يَكُونُ البَحْثُ عَنْ هذاَ البَابِ وَالسُّؤَالُ عَنْهُ وَمَعْرِفَةُ الحَقِّ فِيهِ أَكْبَرَ مَقَاصِدِهِ وَأَعْظَمَ مَطَالِبِهِ ; أَعْنِي بَيَانَ مَا يَنْبَغِي اعْتِقَادُهُ لاَ مَعْرِفَةَ كَيْفِيَّةِ الرَّبِّ وَصِفَاتِهِ. وَلَيْسَتِ النُّفُوسُ الصَّحِيحَةُ إِلَى شَيْءٍ أَشْوَقَ مِنْهاَ إِلَى مَعْرِفَةِ هَذَا الأَمْرِ. وَهَذَا أَمْرٌ مَعْلُومٌ بِالْفِطْرَةِ

الوُجْدِيَّةِ فَكَيْفَ يُتَصَوَّرُ مَعَ قِيَامِ هَذَا المُقْتَضِي - الَّذِي هُوَ مِنْ أَقْوَى المُقْتَضِيَاتِ - أَنْ يَتَخَلَّفَ عَنْهُ مُقْتَضَاهُ فِي أُولَئِكَ السَّادَةِ فِي مَجْمُوعِ عُصُورِهِمْ؟ هَذَا لاَ يَكَادُ يَقَعُ مِنْ أَبْلَدِ الخَلْقِ وَأَشَدِّهِمْ إِعْرَاضاً عَنِ اللهِ وَأَعْظَمِهِمْ إِكْبَابًا عَلَى طَلَبِ الدُّنْيَا وَالْغَفْلَةِ عَنْ ذِكْرِ اللهِ تعالى ; فَكَيْفَ يَقَعُ فِي أُولَئِكَ؟

وَأَمَّا كَوْنُهُمْ كَانُوا مُعْتَقِدِينَ فِيهِ غَيْرَ الحَقِّ أَوْ قَائِلِيهِ: فَهَذَا لاَ يَعْتَقِدُهُ مُسْلِمٌ وَلا عَاقِلٌ عَرَفَ حَالَ القَوْمِ. ثُمَّ الكَلامُ عَنْهُمْ فِي هَذَا البَابِ أَكْثَرُ مِنْ أَنْ يُمْكِنَ سَطْرُهُ فِي هَذِهِ الفَتْوَى أَوْ أَضْعَافِهَا يَعْرِفُ ذَلِك مَنْ طَلَبَهُ وَتَتَبَّعَهُ وَلا يَجُوزُ أَيْضًا أَنْ يَكُونَ الخَالِفُونَ أَعْلَمَ مِنَ السَّالِفِينَ كَمَا يَقُولُهُ بَعْضُ الأَغْبِيَاءِ مِمَّنْ لَمْ يُقَدِّرْ قَدْرَ السَّلَفِ ; بَلْ وَلا عَرَفَ اللهَ وَرَسُولَهُ وَالْمُؤْمِنِينَ بِهِ حَقِيقَةَ المَعْرِفَةِ المَأْمُورِ بِهَا : مِنْ أَنَّ " طَرِيقَةَ السَّلَفِ أَسْلَمُ وَطَرِيقَةَ الخَلَفِ أَعْلَمُ وَأَحْكَمُ ". فَإِنَّ هَؤُلاءِ المُبْتَدِعَةَ الَّذِينَ يُفَضِّلُونَ طَرِيقَةَ الْخَلَفِ مِنَ المُتَفَلْسِفَةِ وَمَنْ حَذَا حَذْوَهُمْ عَلَى طَرِيقَةِ السَّلَفِ : إِنَّمَا أُتُوا مِنْ حَيْثُ ظَنُّوا : أَنَّ طَرِيقَةَ السَّلَفِ هِيَ مُجَرَّدُ الإِيمَانِ بِأَلْفَاظِ القُرْآنِ وَالْحَدِيثِ مِنْ غَيْرِ فِقْهٍ لِذَلِكَ بِمَنْزِلَةِ الأُمِّيِّينَ الَّذِينَ قَالَ فِيهِم : { وَمِنْهُم أُمِيُّونَ لا يَعْلَمُونَ الكِتَابَ إِلّا أَمَانِيّ } وَأَنَّ طَرِيقَةَ الخَلَفِ هِيَ اسْتِخْرَاجُ مَعَانِي النُّصُوصِ المَصْرُوفَةِ عَنْ حَقَائِقِهَا بِأَنْوَاعِ المَجَازَاتِ وَغَرَائِبِ اللُّغَاتِ . فَهَذَا الظَّنُّ الفَاسِدُ أَوْجَبَ تِلْكَ المَقَالَةَ الَّتِي مَضْمُونُهَا نَبْذُ الإِسْلامِ

وَرَاءَ الظَّهْرِ وَقَدْ كَذَبُوا عَلَى طَرِيقَةِ السَّلَفِ وَضَلُّوا فِي تَصْوِيبِ طَرِيقَةِ الخَلَفِ ؛ فَجَمَعُوا بَيْنَ الجَهْلِ بِطَرِيقَةِ السَّلَفِ فِي الكَذِبِ عَلَيْهِمْ، وبيَنَ الجهْلِ وَالضَّلالِ بِتصوْيبِ طَرِيقَةِ الخَلَفِ.

وَسَبَبُ ذَلِكَ اعْتِقَادُهُمْ أَنَّهُ لَيْسَ فِي نَفْسِ الأَمْرِ صِفَةٌ دَلَّتْ عَلَيْهَا هَذِهِ النُّصُوصُ لِلشُّبُهَاتِ الفَاسِدَةِ الَّتِي شَارَكُوا فِيهَا إِخْوَانَهُمْ مِنَ الكَافِرِينَ ؛ فَلَمَّا اعْتَقَدُوا انْتِفَاءَ الصِّفَاتِ فِي نَفْسِ الأَمْرِ وَكَانَ مَعَ ذَلِكَ لَا بُدَّ لِلنَّصوصِ مِنْ مَعْنًى بَقُوا مُتَرَدِّدِينَ بَيْنَ الإِيمَانِ بِاللَّفْظِ وَتَفْوِيضِ الْمَعْنى - وَهِيَ الَّتِي يُسَمُّونَهَا طَرِيقَةَ السَّلَفِ - وَبَيْنَ صَرْفِ اللَّفْظِ إِلَى مَعَانٍ بِنَوْعِ تَكَلُّفٍ - وَهِيَ الَّتِي يُسَمُّونَهَا طَرِيقَةَ الخَلَفِ - فَصَارَ هَذَا البَاطِلُ مُرَكَّبًا مِنْ فَسَادِ العَقْلِ وَالْكُفْرِ بِالسَّمْعِ ؛ فَإِنَّ النَّفْيَ إِنَّمَا اعْتَمَدُوا فِيهِ عَلَى أُمُورٍ عَقْلِيَّةٍ ظَنُّوهَا بَيِّنَاتٍ وَهِيَ شُبُهَاتٌ وَالسَّمْعَ حَرَّفُوا فِيهِ الْكَلامَ عَنْ مَوَاضِعِهِ . فَلَمَّا انْبَنَى أَمْرُهُم عَلَى هَاتَيْنِ الْمُقَدِّمَتَيْنِ الكُفْرِيَّتَيْنِ كَانَتِ النَّتِيجَةُ اسْتِجْهَالَ السَّابِقِينَ الأَوَّلِينَ وَاسْتِبْلاهَهُمْ وَاعْتِقَادَ أَنَّهُمْ كَانُوا قَوْمًا أُمِّيِّينَ بِمَنْزِلَةِ الصَّالِحِينَ مِنَ العَامَّةِ ؛ لَمْ يَتَبَحَّرُوا فِي حَقَائِقِ العِلْمِ بِاللهِ وَلَمْ يَتَفَطَّنُوا لِدَقَائِقِ العِلْمِ الإِلَهِيِّ وَأَنَّ الخَلَفَ الفُضَلاءَ حَازُوا قَصَبَ السَّبْقِ فِي هَذَا كُلِّهِ. ثُمَّ هَذَا القَوْلُ إِذَا تَدَبَّرَهُ الإِنْسَانُ وَجَدَهُ فِي غَايَةِ الجَهَالَةِ ؛ بَلْ فِي غَايَةِ الضَّلالَةِ.

كَيْفَ يَكُونُ هَؤُلاءِ المُتَأَخِّرُونَ - لاَ سِيَّمَا وَالإِشَارَةُ بِالْخَلَفِ إِلَى ضَرْبٍ مِنَ المُتَكَلِّمِينَ الَّذِينَ كَثُرَ فِي بَابِ الدِّينِ اضْطِرَابُهُمْ وَغَلُظَ عَنْ مَعْرِفَةِ اللهِ حِجَابُهُمْ وَأَخْبَرَ الوَاقِفُ عَلَى نِهَايَةِ إِقْدَامِهِمْ بِمَا انْتَهَى إِلَيْهِ مِنْ مَرامِهِم حَيْثُ يَقُولُ: لَعَمْرِي لَقَدْ طُفْتُ المَعَاهِدَ كُلَّهَا وسَيَّرْتُ طَرْفِي بَيْنَ تِلْكَ المَعَالِمِ فَلَمْ أَرَ إِلاَّ وَاضِعاً كَفَّ حَائِرٍ على ذَقَنٍ أَوْ قَارِعًا سِنَّ نَادِمِ. وَأَقَرُّوا عَلَى نُفُوسِهِمْ بِمَا قَالُوهُ مُتَمَثِّلِينَ بِهِ أَوْ مُنْشِئِينَ لَهُ فِيمَا صَنَّفُوهُ مِنْ كُتُبِهِمْ كَقَوْلِ بَعْضِ رُؤَسَائِهِمْ. نِهَايَةُ إِقْدَامِ العُقُولِ عِقَالُ وَأَكْثَرُ سَعْيِ العَالَمِينَ ضَلاَلُ وَأَرْوَاحُنَا فِي وَحْشَةٍ مِنْ جُسُومِنَا وَحاصِلُ دُنْيَانَا أَذًى وَوَبَالُ وَلَمْ نَسْتَفِدْ مِنْ بَحْثِنَا طُولَ عُمْرِنَا سِوَى أَنْ جَمَعْنَا فِيهِ قِيلَ وَقَالُوا. لَقَدْ تَأَمَّلْتُ الطُّرُقَ الكَلامِيَّةَ وَالْمَنَاهِجَ الفَلْسَفِيَّةَ ; فَمَا رَأَيْتُهَا تَشْفِي عَلِيلاً وَلا تُرْوِي غَلِيلاً وَرَأَيْتُ أَقْرَبَ الطُّرُقِ طَرِيقَةَ القُرْآنِ. أَقْرَأُ فِي الإِثْبَاتِ: {الرَّحْمنُ عَلَى العَرْشِ اسْتَوى} {إِلَيْهِ يَصْعَدُ الكَلِمُ الطَّيِّبُ} وَأَقْرَأُ فِي النَّفْي: {لَيْسَ كَمِثْلِهِ شَيْءٌ} {ولا يُحِيطُونَ بِهِ عِلْماً} وَمَنْ جَرَّبَ مِثْلَ تَجْرِبَتِي عَرَفَ مِثْلَ مَعْرِفَتِي ا هـ.

وَيَقُولُ الآخَرُ مِنْهُمْ: لَقَدْ خُضْتُ البَحْرَ الخِضَمَّ وَتَرَكْتُ أَهْلَ الإِسْلامِ وَعُلُومَهُمْ وَخُضْتُ فِي الَّذِي نَهَوْنِي عَنْهُ وَالآنَ إِنْ لَمْ يَتَدَارَكْنِي رَبِّي بِرَحْمَتِهِ فَالْوَيْلُ لِفُلانٍ وَهَا أَنَا أَمُوتُ عَلَى عَقِيدَةِ أُمِّي ا هـ.

وَيَقُولُ الآخَرُ مِنْهُمْ: أَكْثَرُ النَّاسِ شَكًّا عِنْدَ المَوْتِ أَصْحَابُ الكَلامِ. ثُمَّ هَؤُلاءِ المُتَكَلِّمُونَ المُخَالِفُونَ لِلسَّلَفِ إِذَا حُقِّقَ عَلَيْهِمُ الأَمْرُ : لَمْ يُوجَدْ عِنْدَهُمْ مِنْ حَقِيقَةِ العِلْمِ بِاللهِ وَخَالِصِ المَعْرِفَةِ بِهِ خَبَرٌ وَلَمْ يقعوا مِنْ ذَلِكَ عَلَى عَيْنٍ وَلا أَثَرٍ كَيْفَ يَكُونُ هَؤُلاءِ المَحْجُوبُونَ المَنْقُوصُونَ المَسْبُوقُونَ الحَيَارَى المُتَهَوِّكُونَ : أَعْلَمَ بِاللهِ وَأَسْمَائِهِ وَصِفَاتِهِ وَأَحْكَمَ فِي بَابِ ذَاتِهِ وَآيَاتِهِ مِنَ السَّابِقِينَ الأَوَّلِينَ مِنَ المُهَاجِرِينَ وَالأَنْصَارِ وَالَّذِينَ اتَّبَعُوهُمْ بِإِحْسَانٍ مِنْ وَرَثَةِ الأَنْبِيَاءِ وَخُلَفَاءِ الرُّسُلِ وَأَعْلامِ الهُدَى وَمَصَابِيحِ الدُّجَى الَّذِينَ بِهِمْ قَامَ الكِتَابُ وَبِهِ قَامُوا وَبِهِمْ نَطَقَ الكِتَابُ وَبِهِ نَطَقُوا الَّذِينَ وَهَبَهُمُ اللهُ مِنَ العِلْمِ وَالْحِكْمَةِ مَا بَرَّزُوا بِهِ عَلَى سَائِرِ أَتْبَاعِ الأَنْبِيَاءِ فَضْلاً عَنْ سَائِرِ الأُمَمِ الَّذِينَ لاَ كِتَابَ لَهُمْ وَأَحَاطُوا مِنْ حَقَائِقِ المَعَارِفِ وَبَوَاطِنِ الحَقَائِقِ بِمَا لَوْ جُمِعَتْ حِكْمَةُ غَيْرِهِمْ إِلَيْهَا لاسْتَحْيَا مَنْ يَطْلُبُ المُقَابَلَةَ ثُمَّ كَيْفَ يَكُونُ خَيْرُ قُرُونِ الأُمَّةِ أَنْقَصَ فِي العِلْمِ وَالْحِكْمَةِ - لاَ سِيَّمَا العِلْمُ بِاللهِ وَأَحْكَامِ أَسْمَائِهِ وَآيَاتِهِ - مِنْ هَؤُلاءِ الأَصَاغِرِ بِالنِّسْبَةِ إِلَيْهِمْ ؟ أَمْ كَيْفَ يَكُونُ أَفْرَاخُ المُتَفَلْسِفَةِ وَأَتْبَاعُ الهِنْدِ وَالْيُونَانِ وَوَرَثَةُ المَجُوسِ وَالْمُشْرِكِينَ وضُلاَّلُ اليَهُودِ وَالنَّصَارَى والصَّابِئِينَ وَأَشْكَالُهُمْ وَأَشْبَاهُهُمْ أَعْلَمَ بِاللهِ مِنْ وَرَثَةِ الأَنْبِيَاءِ وَأَهْلِ القُرْآنِ وَالإِيمَانِ. وَإِنَّمَا قَدَّمْتُ هَذِهِ المُقَدِّمَةَ لأَنَّ مَن اسْتَقَرَّتْ هَذِهِ المُقَدِّمَةُ عِنْدَهُ عَرَفَ طَرِيقَ الهُدَى أَيْنَ هُوَ فِي هَذَا البَابِ وَغَيْرِهِ وَعَلِمَ أَنَّ الضَّلالَ

والتَّهَوُّكَ إِنَّمَا اسْـتَوْلَى عَلَى كَثِيرٍ مِنَ الْمُتَأَخِّرِينَ بِنَبْذِهِمْ كِتَابَ اللهِ وَرَاءَ ظُهُورِهِمْ وَإِعْرَاضِهِمْ عَمَّا بَعَثَ اللهُ بِهِ مُحَمَّدًا صلى الله عليه وسلم مِنَ الْبَيِّنَاتِ وَالْهُدَى وَتَرْكِهِم الْبَحْثَ عَنْ طَرِيقَةِ السَّـابِقِينَ وَالتَّابِعِينَ وَالْتِمَاسِـهِمْ عِلْمَ مَعْرِفَةِ اللهِ مِمَّنْ لَمْ يَعْرِفِ اللهَ بِإِقْرَارِهِ عَلَى نَفْسِـهِ وَبِشَـهَادَةِ الأُمَّةِ عَلَى ذَلِك وَبِدَلالاتٍ كَثِيرَةٍ ; وَلَيْسَ غَرَضِي وَاحِدًا مُعَيَّنًا وَإِنَّمَا أَصِفُ نَوْعَ هَؤُلاءِ وَنَوْعَ هَؤُلاءِ .

Glossary

A

Āyah: (pl. *āyāt*) "sign," a verse of the *Qur'ān*.
Āhād: a narration which has not reached the level of *mutawātir*.
Ahādīth: see *hadīth*.
'Alayhis-salām: "may Allāh (سُبْحَانَهُ وَتَعَالَىٰ) protect and preserve him." It is said after the name of a Prophet of Allāh or after the name of an Angel.
Anṣār: "helpers;" the Muslims of al-Madīnah who supported the Muslims who migrated from Makkah.
'Arsh: Throne of Allāh (جَلَّ جَلَالُهُ).
'**Aṣr:** the afternoon Prayer.
Awliyā': see *Walī*.

B

Bid'ah: Heresy (any innovatory practice).
Burāq: An animal-bigger than a donkey and smaller than a horse on which the Prophet (صَلَّى ٱللَّهُ عَلَيْهِ وَعَلَىٰ آلِهِ وَسَلَّمَ) went for the *Mi'rāj*.

D

Dā'ī: one engaged in *da'wah*, caller.
Da'īf: "weak," unauthentic narration.

Da'wah: invitation, call to Allāh (عَزَّوَجَلَّ).
Dīn: a completed way of life prescribed by Allāh (تَبَارَكَ وَتَعَالَىٰ).
Dhikr: (pl. *adhkār*) remembrance of Allāh (جَلَّ وَعَلَا) with the heart, sayings of the tongue and actions of our limbs.

E

Īmān: faith, to affirm all that was revealed to the Prophet (صَلَّى ٱللَّهُ عَلَيْهِ وَسَلَّمَ).

F

Fāhish: one who uses foul language.
Fard Kifāyah: collective obligation - if fulfilled by a part of the community then the rest are not obligated.
Fatwā: (pl. *fatāwā*) religious verdicts.
Faqīh: A scholar who can give religious verdicts.
Fiqh: Islāmic jurisprudence, understanding.
Fitnah: (pl. *fitan*) Trials, persecution, conflicts and strife.
Fitrah: the natural-disposition that one is born upon.

G

Ghulū: going to an extreme.
Ghusl: A ceremonial-bath necessary for the one who is in a state of *Janābah*.

H

Hadīth: (pl. *ahādīh*) the saying, actions and approvals narrated from the Prophet (صَلَّى ٱللَّٰهُ عَلَيْهِ وَعَلَىٰ آلِهِ وَسَلَّمَ).
Halāl: lawful.
Hanīf: pure Islāmic Monotheism (worshipping Allāh alone and nothing else).
Harām: unlawful and forbidden.
Hasan: fine, good; a term used for an authentic *hadīth*, which does not reach the level of *Sahīh*.
Harj: killing.
Al-Harūriyyah: an especially un-orthodox religious sect that branched off from the *Khawārij*.
Hijrahh: migration from the land of *Shirk* to the land of Islām.
Hukm: a judgment of legal-decision (especially of Allāh).

I

'Ibādah: worship, worship of Allāh.
Ihsān: worshipping Allāh as though you see Him. However, since you cannot see Him, then know that He sees you.
Ijmā': consensus, a unified opinion of Scholars regarding a certain issue.
Ijtihād: exertion of effort; the process of arriving at a reasoned decision by a Scholar on an issue.
Imām: leaders; leaders in Prayer, knowledge in *fiqh*, leader of a state.
Isnād: the chain of narrators linking the collector of the saying to the person quoted.

Istikhārah: a Prayer consisting of two units (*rak'ah*) asking Allāh for guidance.
Istiwā: ascending; the ascending of Allāh above the Throne (in the manner that befits His Majesty).

J

Janābah: state of a person after having sexual-intercourse or sexual-discharge.
Janāzah: (pl. *janā'iz*): Funeral.
Jihād: striving, struggling, fighting to make the Word of Allāh supreme.
Jum'ah: Friday.
Jinn: invisible creation, created by Allāh from smokeless fire.
Junub: a person who is in the state of *janābah.*

K

Ka'bah: a square stone building in *al-Masjidul-Haram* (the great mosque in Makkah which Muslims go to for pilgrimage and which all Muslims direct their face in Prayer).
Al-Kabā'ir: the major sins.
Khārijī: (pl. *Khawārij*): those who declared that a Muslim becomes a disbeliever due to committing a major sin alone.
Khalīfah: (pl. *khulafā'*): the head of the Islāmic government to whom the oath of allegiance is given.
Khilāfah: an Islāmic state.
Khutbah: (person *khatīb)*, religious talk (sermon).
Kufr: (person *kāfir*) act of disbelief in the Religion of Islām.

M

Madhhab: position or opinion of a Scholar; school of Islāmic Jurisprudence.
Makrūh: not approved of, undesirable from the point of view of Religion, although not punishable.
Manhaj: way; method; methodology.
Marfū': raised; a narration attributed to the Prophet (صَلَّىٰٱللَّهُعَلَيْهِوَسَلَّمَ).
Masjid: mosque.
Mawbiqāt: great destructive sins.
Mudallis: one who practises *tadlīs*.
Muhājir: (pl. *muhājirūn, muhājirīn*) one who migrated from the land of the disbelievers to the land of the Muslims for the sake of Allāh.
Muhaddith: scholar of the science of *hadīth*.
Muftī: one who gives *fatāwā*.
Mujāhid: (pl. *mujāhidūn*): a Muslim warrior in *Jihād*.
Mujtahid: one who is qualified to pass judgment using *ijtihād*.
Munkar: "rejected;" a narration which is un-authentic itself and contradicts and authentic narrations.
Muqallid: one who practices *taqlīd*.
Mushrik: (pl. *mushrikūn*) polytheists, pagans and disbelievers in the oneness of Allāh (عَزَّوَجَلَّ) and His Messenger (صَلَّىٰٱللَّهُعَلَيْهِوَعَلَىٰآلِهِوَسَلَّمَ).
Mustahabb: recommended; an action if left it is not punishable and if done it is rewardable.
Muttaqūn: those who are pious.

Mutawātir: a *hadīth* which is narrated by a very large number of narrators, such that it cannot be supported that they all agreed upon a lie.
Muwahhid: (pl. *muwahhidūn*) one who unifies all of his worship and directs it to Allāh alone.
Mawdū': fabricated; spurious; invented (narration).
Mawqūf: stopped; a narration from a Companion (not going back to the Prophet (صَلَّى ٱللَّهُ عَلَيْهِ وَسَلَّمَ)).
Mawsūl: "connected;" a continuous *isnād* (can be narrated back to the Prophet (صَلَّى ٱللَّهُ عَلَيْهِ وَسَلَّمَ)).

N

Nāfilah: (pl. *nawāfil*) Optional-practice of worship.
Niyyah: intention from the heart.
Nusuk: a sacrifice.

Q

Qadar: Divine pre-ordainment; that which Allāh has ordained for his creation.
Qiblah: the direction the Muslims face during Prayer.
Qiyās: analogical-deduction of Islāmic laws. New laws are deduced from old laws based upon similarity between their causes.
Qunūt: "devotion;" a special-supplication while standing in the Prayer.

Quraysh: one of the greatest tribes in Arabia in the pre-Islāmic period of Ignorance. The Prophet (صَلَّى ٱللَّهُ عَلَيْهِ وَسَلَّمَ) belonged to this tribe.

R

Rāfidī: the correct title for the extreme *Shī'ah.* Those who bear m'Alīce and grudges against the noble Companions (رَضِيَ ٱللَّهُ عَنْهُمْ) to the extent that they declare them to be apostates. They also hold that the *Qur'ān* which the Muslims have is neither complete nor preserved from corruption.

Ramadān: the ninth month of Islāmic calendar, in which Muslims observe fasting.

S

Sahābah: Muslims who met the Prophet (صَلَّى ٱللَّهُ عَلَيْهِ وَسَلَّمَ) believing in him and died believing in him.

Sahīh: authentic, the highest rank of classification of authentic *ahādīth.*

Salaf/Salafus-Sālihīn: pious predecessors; the Muslims of the first three generations: the Companions, the successors and their successors.

Salafī: one who ascribes oneself to the *salaf* and follows their way.

Sīrah: the life story of the Prophet (صَلَّى ٱللَّهُ عَلَيْهِ وَعَلَىٰ آلِهِ وَسَلَّمَ).

Sharī'ah: the divine code of law of Islām.

Shawwāl: the month after *Ramadān.*

Shaytān: Satan

Shī'ah: (see *Rāfidī*) a collective name for various sects claiming love for *Ahl al-Bayt*.
Shirk: associating partners with Allāh directly or indirectly; compromising any aspects of *Tawhīd*.
Sūrah: a chapter of the *Qur'ān*
Sunnah : "example, practice;" the way of life of the Prophet (صَلَّى ٱللَّٰهُ عَلَيْهِ وَسَلَّمَ), consisting of his words, actions and silent approvals. The *Sunnah* is contained in various *ahādīth*.

T

Tābi'ī: (pl. *Tābi'īn*) the generation that came after the Companions of the Prophet (صَلَّى ٱللَّٰهُ عَلَيْهِ وَسَلَّمَ).
Tafsīr: explanation of the *Qur'ān*.
Tāghūt: anything worshiped other than the real-God (Allāh) (i.e. false deities).
Tahajjud: voluntary, recommended Prayer between the compulsory prayers of *'Ishā'* and *Fajr*.
Takhrīj: to reference a *hadīth* to its sources and analyze its *isnāds*.
Taqlīd: blind following; to follow someone's opinion (*madhhab*) without evidence.
Taqwā: acting in obedience to Allāh, hoping for His mercy upon light from Him and *taqwā* is leaving acts of disobedience, out of fear of Him, upon light from Him.
Tarjamah: notes about a reporter of *hadīth*.
Tawwāf: the circumambulation of the *Ka'bah*.
Tawhīd: Islāmic Monotheism. The Oneness of Allāh. Believing and acting upon His Lordship, His rights of Worship and Names and Attributes.

U

Uhud: A well known mountain in al-Madīnah. One of the greatest battles in Islāmic history came at its foot. This is called *Ghazwah Uhud.*
'Ulamā': (singular: *'ālim*) scholars.
Umm: mother of, used as an identification.
Ummah [nation]: "nation", the Muslims as a whole.
'Umrah: a visit to Makkah during which one performs the *tawwāf* around the *Ka'bah* and the *Sa'ī* between *al-Safā* and *al-Marwah.* It is called the lesser *Hajj.*
Usūl: the fundamentals.

W

Wahyī: the revelation or inspiration of Allāh to His Prophets.
Wahdatul-Wujūd: the belief that everything in existence is infact Allāh. This deviant belief is held by many *Sūfīs.*
Wakīl: disposer of affairs.
Witr: "odd;" the last Prayer at the night, which consists of odd number of *raka'āt* (units).
Walīmah: the wedding feast.
Wasīlah: the means of approach or achieving His closeness to Allāh by getting His favors.
Wudū': an ablution (ritual-washing) that is performed before Prayer and other kinds of worship.

Y

Yaqīn: perfect absolute faith.
Yathrib: one of the names of al-Madīnah.

Z

Zakāt: charity that is obligatory on everyone who has wealth over and above a certain limit over which a year has passed (2.5% of saved wealth).
Zakātul-Fitr: an obligatory charity by the Muslims to be given to the poor before the Prayer of *'Īd al-Fitr*.
Zamzam: the sacred water inside the *haram* (the grand mosque) at Makkah.
Zanādiqah: atheists, heretics.

OUR CALL TO THE UMMAH

[1]: We believe in Allāh and His Names and Attributes, as they were mentioned in the Book of Allāh and in the *Sunnah* of the Messenger of Allāh (عَزَّوَجَلَّ), without *taḥrīf* (distortion), nor *ta'wīl* (figurative interpretation), nor *tamthīl* (making a likeness), nor *tashbīh* (resemblance), nor *ta'ṭīl* (denial).

[2]: We love the Companions (رَضِيَ ٱللَّهُ عَنْهُمْ) of the Messenger of Allaah (صَلَّى ٱللَّهُ عَلَيْهِ وَسَلَّمَ), and we hate those who speak against them. We believe that to speak ill of them is to speak ill of the Religion, because they are the ones who conveyed it to us. And we love the Family of the Prophet (صَلَّى ٱللَّهُ عَلَيْهِ وَسَلَّمَ) with love that is permitted by the *Sharī'ah*. 'Imrān Ibn Ḥusayn (رَضِيَ ٱللَّهُ عَنْهُ) said, "O people! Learn the knowledge of the Religion from us, if you do not do so, then you will certainly be misguided."

[3]: We love the People of *Ḥadīth* and all of the *Salaf* of the *Ummah* from *Ahl al-Sunnah*. Imām al-Shāṭibī (d.790H) - رَحِمَهُ ٱللَّهُ - said, "The *Salaf al-Ṣāliḥ*, the Companions, the *tābi'īn* and their successors knew the *Qur'ān*, its sciences and its meanings the best."

[4]: We despise *'ilm al-kalām* (knowledge of theological-rhetoric), and we view it to be from amongst the greatest reasons for the division in the *Ummah*.

[5]: We do not accept anything from the books of *fiqh* (jurisprudence), nor from the books of *tafsīr* (explanation of the *Qur'ān*), nor from the ancient stories, nor from the *Sīrah* (biography) of the Prophet (صَلَّى ٱللَّهُ عَلَيْهِ وَسَلَّمَ), except that which has been confirmed from Allāh or from His Messenger (صَلَّى ٱللَّهُ عَلَيْهِ وَسَلَّمَ). We do not mean that we have rejected them, nor do we claim that we are not in need

of them. Rather, we benefit from the discoveries of our Scholars and the jurists and other than them. However, we do not accept a ruling, except with an authentic proof.

[6]: We do not write in our books, nor do we cover in our lessons, nor do we give sermons with anything except the *Qur'ān*, or the authentic and authoritative *ḥadīth*. And we detest what emanates from many books and admonishers in terms of false stories and weak and fabricated *aḥādīth*. 'Abdullāh Ibn al-Mubārak (d.181H) - رَحِمَهُ ٱللَّهُ - said, "The authentic *aḥādīth* are sufficient and the weak *aḥādīth* are not needed."

[7]: We do not perform *takfīr* upon any Muslim due to any sin, except *Shirk* with Allāh, or the abandonment of Prayer, or apostasy. We seek refuge in Allāh from that.

[8]: We believe that the *Qur'ān* is the Speech of Allāh, it is not created.

[9]: We hold that our 'obligation is to co-operate with the group that traverses the methodology of the Book and the *Sunnah*, and what the *Salaf* of the *Ummah* were upon; in terms of calling to Allāh (سُبْحَانَهُ وَتَعَالَىٰ), and being sincere in worship of Him, and warning from *Shirk*, innovations, and disobedience, and to advise all of the groups that oppose this.' 'So co-operating upon righteousness and piety (*taqwā*) and mutual-advising necessitates warning against evil and not co-operating with the wicked.'

[10]: We do not deem it correct to revolt against the Muslim rulers as long as they are Muslims, nor do we feel that revolutions bring about reconciliation. Rather, they corrupt the community.

[11]: We hold that this multiplicity of present day parties is a reason for the division of the Muslims and their weakness. So therefore we set about 'freeing the minds from the fetters of blind-following and the darkness of sectarianism and party spirit.'

[12]: We restrict our understanding of the Book of Allāh and of the *Sunnah* of the Messenger of Allāh (صَلَّى ٱللَّهُ عَلَيْهِ وَسَلَّمَ) to the understanding of the *Salaf* of the *Ummah* from the Scholars of *ḥadīth*, not the blind-followers of their individuals. Rather, we take the truth from wherever it comes. And we know that there are those who claim *Salafiyyah*, yet *Salafiyyah* is free from them, since they bring to the society what Allāh has prohibited. We believe in 'cultivating the young generation upon this Islām, purified from all that we have mentioned, giving to them a correct Islāmic education from the start - without any influence from the disbelieving western education.'

[13]: We believe that politics is a part of the Religion, and those who try to separate the Religion from politics are only attempting to destroy the Religion and to spread chaos.

[14]: We believe there will be no honour or victory for the Muslims until they return to the Book of Allaah and to the *Sunnah* of the Messenger of Allāh (صَلَّى ٱللَّهُ عَلَيْهِ وَسَلَّمَ).

[15]: We oppose those who divide the Religion into trivialities and important issues. And we know that this is a destructive *da'wah*.

[16]: We oppose those who put down the knowledge of the *Sunnah*, and say that this is not the time for it. Likewise, we oppose those who put down acting upon the *Sunnah* of the Messenger of Allāh (صَلَّى ٱللَّهُ عَلَيْهِ وَسَلَّمَ).

[17]: Our *da'wah* and our *'aqīdah* is more beloved to us than our own selves, our wealth and our offspring. So we are not prepared to part with it for gold, nor silver. We say this so that no one may have hope in buying out our *da'wah*, nor should he think that it is possible for him to purchase it from us for *dīnār* or *dirham*.

[18]: We love the present day Scholars of the *Sunnah* and hope to benefit from them and regret the passing away of many of them. Imām Mālik said (d.179H) - رَحِمَهُ ٱللَّهُ, "The knowledge of *ḥadīth* is your flesh and blood and you will be asked concerning it on the Day of Judgement, so look who you are taking it from."

[19]: We do not accept a *fatwā* except from the Book of Allāh and the *Sunnah* of the Messenger of Allāh (صَلَّى ٱللَّهُ عَلَيْهِ وَسَلَّمَ).

These are glimpses into our *'aqīdah* and our *da'wah*. So if one has any objection to this, then we are prepared to accept advice if it is truthful, and to refute it if it is erroneous, and to avoid it if it is stubborn rejection. And Allāh knows best.